4-98

ROBINSON
606 NORTH STREET
ROBINSON, IL 62454-2699

S0-GGM-122

ROBINSON PUBLIC LIBRARY DIST
606 NORTH JEFFERSON STREET
ROBINSON, IL 62454-2699

DESKTOP PUBLISHING DICTIONARY

Also by Donald D. Spencer and available from Camelot Publishing Company.

Spencer's Illustrated Computer Dictionary
Personal Computer Dictionary
Computer Dictionary, 4th Edition
Illustrated Computer Graphics Dictionary
Exploring Number Theory With Microcomputers, 3rd Edition
Invitation to Number Theory With PASCAL, 2nd Edition
Key Dates In Number Theory History
Computer Mathematics With BASIC Programming
Computer Mathematics With PASCAL Programming
Introduction To Computing With BASIC
Introduction To Computing With TURBO PASCAL
Computer Humor
Understanding Computers, 3rd Edition
Discover Computers
Using Computers

DESKTOP PUBLISHING DICTIONARY

DONALD D. SPENCER, Ph.D.

265 ILLUSTRATIONS

CAMELOT PUBLISHING COMPANY
Ormond Beach, Florida

Published by
CAMELOT PUBLISHING COMPANY
P.O. Box 1357
Ormond Beach, FL 32175

Printed on acid-free paper

Copyright © 1996 by Donald D. Spencer

All rights reserved. No part of this book may be reproduced in any form without the permission of Camelot Publishing Company.

ISBN 0-89218-215-6

Library of Congress Cataloging-in-Publication Data

Spencer, Donald D.
    Desktop publishing dictionary / Donald D. Spencer.
       p.   cm.
    ISBN 0-89218-215-6
    1. Desktop publishing--Dictionaries.   I. Title.
Z253.53.S64 1996
686.2'2544'03--dc20   94-47199
                                                        CIP

PREFACE

There is probably no one event nor single set of circumstances, nor one invention nor method nor process that has had such a profound effect on the production of typographic images as has the microcomputer. Since its introduction in the latter half of the 1970s, it has grown steadily to become a significant publishing tool. Desktop publishing is an indespensible tool for a growing number of publishers, businesses and computer users. With the advent of powerful microcomputers, inexpensive laser printers, and sophisticated publishing software, many organizations now produce newsletters, reports, newspapers, manuals, booklets and books in-house.

The *Desktop Publishing Dictionary* contains 1700 of the most frequently used terms, words, acronymns, and abbreviations involved in desktop publishing. It contains all of the terms that most often confuse a beginner. All definitions are given in clear, easy-to-understand language. In many cases, definitions are supported by illustrations.

This book is intended for several kinds of readers. It is a basic reference book for the person who knows little or nothing about desktop publishing but wants to learn. It is hoped that business people, professionals, writers, publishers, students, teachers, and others will find it a useful source book.

The keynote of this book is clarity, without sacrifice of authority and precision. All definitions are simple and stand as independent units of explanation. Technical terms are kept out of the definitions as much as possible. In a few cases where a special terminology is required, the expressions used are carefully defined, and related terms or concepts are indicated by cross-references.

This book is as up to date and complete as possible. However, new terms and names are constantly being added to the desktop publishing language. These will be collected by the author for possible inclusion in subsequent editions of this book.

The forerunner of the modern book designer - a scribe at his desk working on ruled parchment.

HOW TO USE THIS DICTIONARY

The terms in this dictionary appear in alphabetical order of the complete term (spaces and hyphens don't count); for example, **sidebar** comes between **side** and **side bearing**. This order contrasts with some dictionaries in which the alphabetical order is based on a heavier weighing of the first word in a term; for example, all terms commencing with "side" precede all terms commencing with "sidebar."

All terms listed in the dictionary are in **boldface**. Cross-references that are important to an understanding of any term are given in *italics*.

If you cannot find a word, it might be listed in a slightly different form. For example, you might try looking for "page layout" and find the description under "page design." I have included only one definition to keep from cluttering the book with the obvious.

The terms normally appear in boldface lower case characters. Proper names and nouns are headed by an upper case letter; for example, **Gutenberg, Johann**. Acronyms are presented in boldface caps and the proper letters are amplified in the text; for example, **PDP** stands for Page Description Language.

DESKTOP PUBLISHING DICTIONARY

a.a. Abbreviation for author's alteration. A change in the page proofs, made by the author, which is not part of the manuscript that the author and editor, typesetter or printer have previously approved to have typeset. The author bears the expense of author's alterations over and above a percentage stated in the contract or agreement.

abort Procedure for terminating a program when a mistake, malfunction, or error occurs.

ABI form See *Advanced Book Information form*.

absorption The degree to which colors or chemicals are absorbed by paper.

abstract A brief summary of an article, report or book.

accelerator A device to speed up either the computer or monitor. Typically a circuit card with an extra processing chip and/or additional RAM.

accent face A variation of a standard typeface in exaggerated weight or a radically different form.

accents A special symbol, combined with an alphabetical character, to form a specialized character, primarily for pronunciation and foreign language use.

access (1) Generally, the obtaining of data. To locate desired data. (2) To store on and retrieve data from a disk.

access time Memory access is how fast a character in memory can be transferred to or from the processor. Disk access is an average of how fast the access arm can position the read/write head over the requested track.

achromatic Without color. In printing, refers to the use of black ink on white paper.

acid In chemistry, a substance capable of forming hydrogen ions when dissolved in water. Acids can weaken cellulose in paper, board, and cloth, leading to brittleness. Acids may be introduced in the manufacture of various library materials and may be left in intentionally or incidentally. Acids may also be introduced by migration from other materials or from atmospheric pollution.

acid free paper A type of paper produced from virtually any cellulose fiber source (cotton and wood, among others), if measures are taken during manufacture to eliminate active acid from the pulp. However free of acid a paper may be at the time of manufacture, over time the presence of residual chlorine from bleaching, aluminum sulfate from sizing, or pollutants in the atmosphere may lead to the formation of acid unless the paper has been buffered with an alkaline substance. Also called alkaline paper.

acknowledgments page A page of front matter where the author acknowledges or credits those who helped with the book.

acoustic coupler A type of modem. It translates computer signals into telephone tones and the reverse. This allows computers to communicate with each other by the telephone network.

acquisition librarian A library employee who has the responsibility of ordering new books for the library.

acquisition editor The publishing house editor who specializes in the acquisition rather than the editing of manuscripts.

acronym A word formed from the first letter (or letters) of each word in a phrase or name (e.g. VDT stands for Visual Display Terminal, IC stands for Integrated Circuit, RAM stands for Random-Access Memory and DP stands for Desktop Publishing).

across the grain See *against the grain*.

activate To put a unit or device into an operational state.

active file File currently being used.

active program Any program that is loaded into computer memory and ready to be executed.

active white space White space that separates and organizes design elements.

active window When using a graphics user interface, the active window is the window currently in use.

activity light A small light on the computer's front panel that indicates when a disk drive is reading or writing data.

actual page The page as it is printed.

actual size A display view of a document at the same size it will be printed.

ad An abbreviation for advertisement.

addendum Matter to be included in a book after the body copy has been set, which is printed separately at the beginning or end of the text; something added to a book.

ADEPT Acronym for Association for the Development of Desktop Publishing Techniques, an organization designed to help people involved in electronic publishing.

adhesive binding Alternate term for *perfect binding.*

Adobe Font Metrics (AFM) A specification for storing (in a text file) font metrics information such as character widths, kerning pairs, and character bounding boxes.

Adobe Type Manager A font generator and utility for the Apple Macintosh computer from Adobe Systems Inc.

ADP Acronym for Association of Desktop Publishers, an organization designed to assist members working in the desktop publishing field.

advance Money paid to an author for selling a manuscript or reprint rights to a publisher. The advance is against future royalties.

Advanced Book Information (ABI) form A special book information form sent by the publisher to R.R. Bowker, who uses the information to list books in its directories, i.e., *Books in Print, Forthcoming Books,* etc.

advertisement A notice in a newspaper or magazine.

advertisement page A page of frontmatter where the publisher lists other titles by the author and publisher.

afterword An author's comment to the reader placed in a book's back matter.

against the grain Folding paper at right angles to the grain.

agate A measurement used in typesetting. A measure of 14 agate lines equal one inch. Usually the classified ads of newspapers or magazines are measured in agate lines. Agate type is about 5.5 points in height.

air See *white space*.

aldine type A type somewhat resembling Roman, but heaver in face and somewhat condensed.

Aldus Manutius (1450-1515) A very celebrated publisher and printer at the beginning of the sixteenth century, who practiced his art chiefly in Venice, Italy. He produced his first book in 1495. Thereafter, he was a prolific publisher, especially of classical texts.

Aldus Manutius

Aldus PageMaker A desktop publishing program for IBM-compatible and Apple Macintosh microcomputers. It was introduced in 1985 by Aldus Corporation. This program set the standard for desktop publishing. Paul Brainerd, president of Aldus, coined the term desktop publishing.

aliasing A stepped edge or "staircase" in computer generated images. Appears along lines that are not perfectly horizontal or vertical. Aliasing is especially noticeable in low-resolution monitors.

alignment (1) The way that text lines up on a page or in a column. (2) Positioning characters on a common reference line. Horizontal alignment is based on the baseline. Vertical alignment is based on the margins.

alignment

alkaline paper Alternate term for *acid free paper.*

alley The white space separating columns of type in publication design.

alphabet The characters of a given language, arranged in a traditional order.

ABCDEFGHIJKLMNOPQRSTUVWXYZ
abcdefghijklmnopqrstuvwxyz

alphabet

alphanumeric data Data represented by digits, letters and special characters.

alternate characters Multiple versions of different characters to allow greater variety or personality to copy. "Bookman" was one of the first typefaces to have alternate characters. "Avant Garde" has both alternate characters and alternate combinations of characters.

AABBCDDEEFFGHH
IJKKLLMMNNOP
PQRRSTTUUVVWW
XXYYZ&abcdefghijkl
mnopqrstuvwxyz

alternate characters

American Bookseller's Association (ABA) A professional association serving the needs of the bookseller. ABA holds an annual convention which is the largest English-language gathering of book people in the world. Booksellers are able to see books of virtually all U.S. and many foreign publishers.

American Library Association (ALA) A professional association of librarians and others interested in the working and advancement of libraries.

ampersand (&) Symbol for the Latin word *et*, meaning *and*. Used in titles and company names primarily.

ampersand

annotation Captions used on illustrations or photographs.

anonym A book in which the name of the author does not appear.

anthology A collection of writings by several authors published as a single work.

antialiasing At low resolutions, diagonal lines in digitized images appear as stair-steps and are called "jaggies." This effect is called "aliasing." Antialiasing is the smoothing or removal of these "jaggies" to recreate smoother diagonal lines.

antiquarian bookseller A bookseller who specializes in buying and selling old and rare books.

antique book paper Heavy, tough, anti-glare stock used in printing books.

antique finish Usually applied to book and cover papers with a natural, rough finish.

antivirus program A program designed to counter the effects of a virus program.

apex

apex In typography, where two lines meet at the top of a character, such as in the letter A and the center of the cap W. The opposite of an apex — that is the bottom junction of two lines — is the vortex. The cap W has one apex and two vortex points.

appendix In book typography, the material following the regular text at the end of a book, such as notes, bibliography, glossary and reference materials related to the book.

Apple Computer, Inc.   One of the first and certainly the most influential of the microcomputer manufacturers. Founded in 1976 by Steven P. Jobs and Stephen G. Wozniak, using the family garage as a base and $100 in capital, Apple made computers that became wildly successful. Because of excellent design principles, the early Apple II family of microcomputers is still useful. Later machines, such as the Macintosh family of microcomputers, have become extremely popular and have greatly affected the design of other machines and of software. The Macintosh computer, with its innovative software, is in a class by itself. Apple Computer, Inc. is a leader in high-performance personal computing.

Apple Macintosh   See *Macintosh*.

application   A software program specially designed for particular user needs or the specific use of a software program. Graphics applications are usually designed to enable the user to manipulate data or from a library of shapes or clip art.

application software   Software that is specific to the solution of an application problem. Some examples are word processing programs, electronic spreadsheets, games, educational programs, drawing programs, etc.

archival paper   Acid free paper — a paper that has the ability to resist deterioration for many years.

archival storage   (1) Refers to memory (on magnetic disks, optical disks, or magnetic tape) used to store data outside of the main memory. (2) Saving digital data for future references. (3) A storage system for information designed to be kept for a long period of time.

area composition   The arranging of text and graphic elements on a page for reproduction. The electronic term for **pasteup** or page composition.

area chart   Area charts are usually a combination of two line charts with the difference between the two highlighted to accentuate that difference.

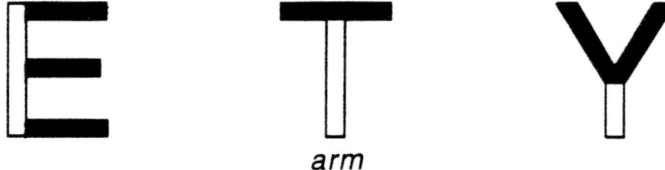
arm

arm   The part or stroke of a letter that extends upward, horizontally as in a T or diagonally up, as the right-top stroke of a K.

armpit A narrow headline immediately under a wider one.

arrows Symbols that indicate direction.

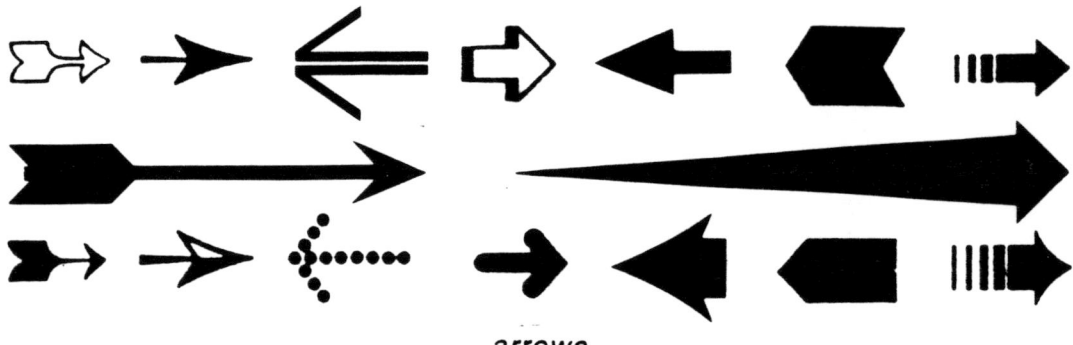

arrows

arrow keys Keyboard keys that are used to move the cursor up, down, left or right on the display screen.

art Refers to the non-typographic elements of a document, such as diagrams, illustrations, photographs, and graphs. Stated in the negative, it is all that is not text.

artwork

artwork (1) Visual and graphic elements on a page, such as line drawings, halftones, or solids. (2) One of the outputs of a graphics system. (3) A general term applied to any artistic production. (4) The finished page of a layout with all the elements (text, graphics) positioned and ready to print.

ascender Portion of lower-case letters that extends above the main portion of the letter, such as the tops of b, d, h, k, l and t.

ascender

ascent A font's maximum distance above the baseline.

ASCII Acronym for American Standard Code for Information Interchange. Pronounced "ask-ee." A 7-bit standard code adopted to facilitate interchange of data among various types of data processing and data communications equipment.

ASCII file A file encoded in the industry standard representation for text, ASCII, containing only plain text and the basic text formatting characters such as spaces and carriage returns. It contains no graphics or special character formatting codes.

aspect ratio The proportions, or height-to-width ratio, of a picture expressed as a fraction. For example, the aspect ratio of a picture measuring four inches high and eight inches wide is 4:8.

Association of American Publishers (AAP) A trade organization of book publishers.

Association of American University Presses (AAUP) A trade organization for publishers of scholarly books from college and university presses.

asterisk (*) A symbol often used to indicate a footnote or give special emphasis.

ATM Acronym for Adobe Type Manager, a program that improves a screen display by imaging fonts directly from their Type 1 PostScript language font files.

attribute (1) The property of a graphic image that determines characteristics such as line type, line width, and color. (2) A character emphasis, such as boldface and italic, or the size and font of the type.

author The originator of a manuscript; and person who writes for publication.

authorized dealer One who is authorized by the manufacturer/developer to sell, service and support its product.

author/publisher See *self publisher.*

author's alteration A change or correction specified by the author.

autoleading The function that automatically adjusts the space between lines of text when the type size is increased or decreased.

automatic backup A software program feature that automatically saves the file you are currently working on under a special name every few minutes.

automatic columns Fitting text into predefined columns.

automatic hyphenation A feature that hyphenates words automatically. Often found in word processing and page layout programs.

automatic pagination A feature that automatically breaks text into pages. Often found in word processing and page layout programs.

automatic reformatting In word processing, automatic adjustment of text to accommodate changes.

autorotation The ability of a printer to rotate fonts and other elements of a page to print in either portrait or landscape mode. See *landscape* and *portrait.*

autotrace A feature of many drawing programs that draws lines along the edges of a bitmapped image in order to convert the image into an object-oriented one. Using the autotrace tool you can transform low-resolution graphics (72 dots per inch bit-mapped image) into art that can print at substantially higher resolution (object-oriented graphics can print at the printer's maximum resolution).

auxiliary storage Storage that supplements the main storage of a computer, such as hard disks, floppy disks, magnetic tapes, and optical disks.

axis A line, either real or imaginary, used to align text or illustrations in a layout.

backbone The back or spine of a bound book.

background The decoration surrounding certain initial letters.

backlist Previously published books available from a publisher. Contrast with *frontlist.*

backmatter Elements of a book after the last chapter. Can include appendices, notes, bibliography, glossary, author's biography, index, etc. Also called "endmatter."

backslant Characters that slant left of the vertical axis (which is opposite of italic). Used primarily for special effects.

backspace Keyboard operation that moves the cursor one place to the left. Allows modification of what has already been typed before it is entered into the computer.

background operations The operations occurring in the background (such as printing a document or performing a series of calculations) while you are working with an application program in the foreground.

backup disk A duplicate copy of a floppy disk that preserves files in case of some disaster.

backward compatible Compatible with earlier versions of a product.

bad break A place where a word, line, or page is improperly divided. For example, an incorrectly hyphenated word or a page beginning or ending with a widow.

bad copy Any manuscript that is illegible, improperly edited, or otherwise unsatisfactory to be typeset.

bad disk A disk that is unusable.

bad sectors During formatting of disks, all sectors are checked for usability. Unusable sectors are "flagged" as bad and are not used by the operating system. The remaining areas can then still be used.

balloon Circle enclosing copy.

ballot box Open square bullet, usually intended to receive a checkmark.

ballpoint pen The ballpoint pen was invented in 1938 by a Hungarian journalist, Laszlo Biro (1899-1985). During a visit to the print shop of the magazine for which he wrote, Biro was impressed by the advantage of quick drying ink. He proceeded to make a prototype of a pen baed on the same principle. To escape the Nazi threat, he settled in Argentina in 1940 and there developed his invention. He patented it on June 10, 1943, and his pens were sold in Buenos Aires from 1945 on.

b&w Abbreviation for black and white.

bank One line of a headline.

banner A large headline or title, often referred to as a masterhead, that extends across the full page, such as the name of a magazine or newspaper. It can also be used to indicate any large headline.

banner

bar The enclosed horizontal stroke in characters like "A," "H," and "e."

bar chart Widely used chart in business graphics. Used to display a time schedule. Bar charts compare adjacent pieces of data and can depict individual data items side by side, stacked on top of one another, clustered together, or positioned horizontally.

bar code Code made up of a series of variable-width vertical lines which can be read by an optical bar reader. Bar codes are used to identify retail sales items, books, etc.

bar code

bargain books The term used by booksellers to describe books sold at a price lower than the original retail price.

bar graph A graph made up of filled-in columns or rows that represent the change of data over time.

baseline

baseline An imaginary horizontal line with which the base of each character, excluding descenders, is aligned.

baseline shift Adjusting the distance of a letter from its baseline. Baseline shift of zero means there is no shift. Usually specified in points or fractions of an em.

basis weight The weight in pounds of one ream (500 sheets) of paper. Each category of paper has its own standard size. Papers used for the pages of a book are usually 25 x 28 inches. Papers used for covers are usually 20 x 26 inches.

bastard type Type in other than a standard point size.

BBS Acronym for Bulletin Board System. Enables users to log into another computer system from remote terminals. Many of these BBS's can be used free of charge and can be reached by modem.

beak The strokes at the ends of arms and serifs, such as in the letters, E, F, G, T, and Z.

Berne Convention International copyright agreement. The Berne Convention was the first systematic attempt to make a general international agreement on copyright.

Bernoulli box A removable hard disk system for microcomputers, manufactured by Iomega Corporation. The main advantage of this cartridge system is that one hard disk system can be used for multiple libraries of hard disk data.

berserk Refers to the fit of rage computer users go into when their computer fails to work the way they thought it would.

bestsellers Books identified as the result of the compilation and analysis of sales recorded by selected booksellers throughout the country and ranked by *The New York Times* and *Publishers Weekly* on a weekly basis.

Bezier curve A type of curve generated by an algorithm. Named after French mathematician Pierre Bezier., it is used to display nonuniform curves based upon a fitting algorithm. Bezier curves need only a few points to define a large number of shapes, hence their usefulness over other mathematical methods for approximating a given shape. Within drawing programs, Bezier curves are typically reshaped by moving the handles that appear off of the curve. Originated around 1962 for use in car body design in France.

bf An abbreviation used to mark copy that should be set in boldface type.

bible stock Special thin opaque paper used for printing bibles, dictionaries and other massive books.

bibliography A section of backmatter listing books and other publications relevant to the book.

Bic ballpoint pen In 1953 a French baron, Bich, developed an industrial process for manufacturing ballpoint pens that dramatically lowered the cost of production. The Bic was born, and each year people buy three billion of them.

bidirectional printer Printer that prints from left to right as well as from right to left, avoiding carriage-return delay.

biform Refers to the intermingling of modified small cap and lowercase characters in the formation of a lowercase alphabet. Type set with such characters has a unique appearance. The most famous biform face is "Peignot." Biforms are most often used in heads or subheads or advertising display.

binary Mathematical representation of a number to the base 2, i.e., with only two states, 1 and 0; ON and OFF: or HIGH and LOW. Requires a greater number of digits than base 10, i.e. 254 = 11111110.

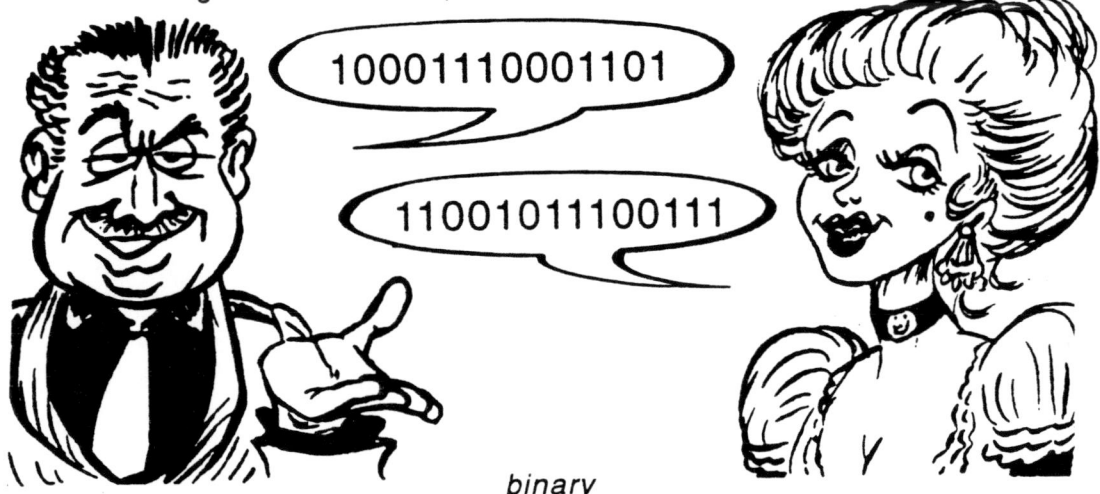

binary

binder's boards Heavyweight cardboard around which the cover is wrapped to form the book's case.

binding The method for holding together pages of a document. Common methods are drilling or punching for a binder, plastic comb, saddle stitching, and perfect binding.

binding margin The space added to the side of the page that will be bound or drilled. Usually added to the left side of right pages and the right side of left pages.

bit The smallest unit of information that can be stored and processed by a computer.

bit flipping Process of inverting bits — changing 1's to 0's and vice versa. For example, in a graphics program, to invert a black-and-white bit-mapped image (to change black to white and vice versa), the program could simply flip the bits that makeup the bit map.

bit mapped font A set of characters in a particular size and style, in which each character is described in a unique bit map (pattern of dots). Bit mapped screen or printer fonts represent characters with a matrix of dots. To display or print bit mapped fonts, the computer or printer must keep a full representation of each character in memory.

bit mapped graphics A method of generating screen images by creating a one-for-one correspondence between bits in memory and pixels on the screen. In color graphics, three or more bits are required in the bit map to represent the red, green, and blue values of an individual pixel. Bit mapped graphics are created by paint programs and some scanners.

bit-mapped graphics

black and white photograph A photo made using a medium that reproduces images with varying shades of gray only, as compared to a color photograph.

black letter

black letter A family of typefaces derived from German handwriting of the medieval era. Black letter typefaces often are called Fraktur because the medieval scribes who created this design lifted their pens from the line to form the next character — fracturing the continuous flow of handwriting. Old English, Gothic, and Fraktur are commonly used type families in this group.

black-writing A mode of laser printer operation in which the laser beam defines the black aspect of an image. White-writing refers to a system whereby the laser removes black to build an image on the printer's drum.

bleed An image on a printed page that runs off the page (no margins).

blend A feature on many digital painting programs that lets you soften the edges or mix colors where two objects or regions meet.

blind folio A page without a printed page number. For example, the front pages of many books.

block letter A letter created with equal stroke weights and simple curves.

block marking The process of indicating a portion of text either by reverse video or an alternate color.

blow-up (1) The changing of a smaller format picture into a larger format picture. (2) Unexpected halt to a program due to a bug or because it encounters data conditions it cannot handle.

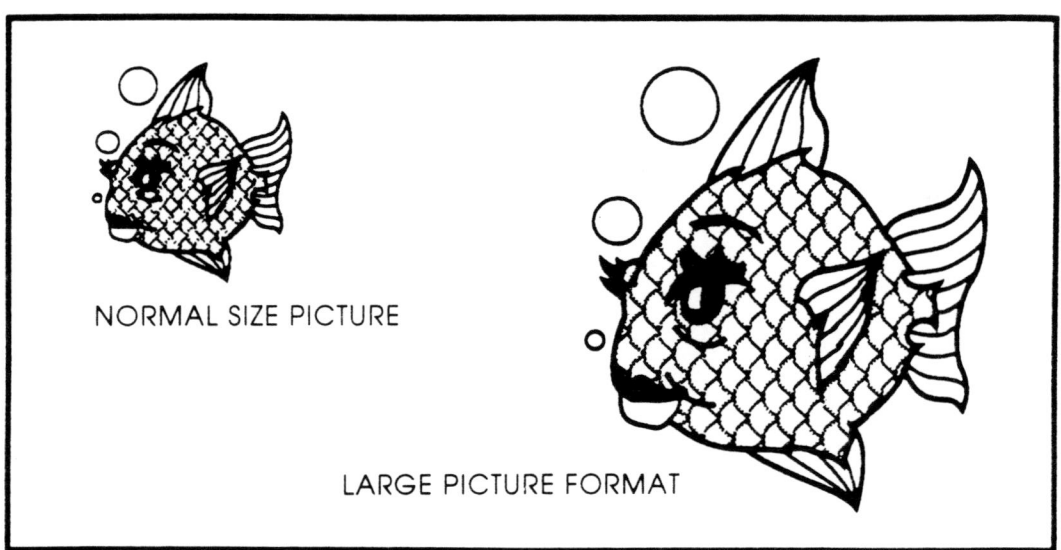

blow-up

blueline A photocopy of the film from which the printer will make the final plates for printing, printed in blue.

blur To reduce contrast on a photograph in a computer file.

blurb A short summary of the contents of a book to be used as advertising copy.

body copy Blocks of type other than the headline or display type. Usually smaller than 14 point. Also called body text.

body size The type's point size which is determined by measuring from the highest ascender to the lowest descender (plus any additional white space to the descender line).

body size

body type Type (usually from 6 point to 14 point) used for lengthy composition; type used for the main text of typeset material, in contrast to headlines and captions — the bulk of the text in a publication. Also called *text type*.

boilerplate Text, graphics, or a page layout that is used over and over again with no or few changes in different documents.

boldface A type font in which the main strokes of the letter are thicker than normal. Printed characters in darker type than the surrounding characters.

NORMAL TYPE ABCDEFGHIJKLMNOPQRSTUVWXYZ 1234567890 ($%£) .;!-?:,"*"

BOLD TYPE ABCDEFGHIJKLMNOPQRSTUVWXYZ 1234567890 ($%£)

boldface

bomb (1) A concealed fault that can cause a system to crash. (2) To sabotage a system by deliberately writing a program that will disrupt the system. (3) To fail suddenly and completely. See *crash*.

book (1) The medium weight of a typeface intended for text use. (2) Set of printed sheets bound in any form of squared binding such as perfect, case, or comb.

bookbinding Protective cover of a book and the process of making it. Reduced to its essentials, a bookbinding is the outer covering of a book, attached to the book itself by adhesive or stitching. See *casebound* and *perfect binding*.

book fair A gathering of book lovers at which book publishers rent tables or booths to display and sell their books. See *Frankfurt Book Fair*.

book history Although the book first appeared in China in the 2nd millenium B.C., it was only between the 2nd and 4th centuries A.D. that it appeared in the West in the form we know. During this period, it went from being the volume (a scroll of papyrus or parchment), which was not very manageable, to the more portable form of sheets bound together. See *papyrus* and *parchment*.

booklet A saddle-stitched volume of less than 64 pages.

booklet

book library The first libraries appeared in Chaldea in 1700 B.C.; the "books" were baked clay tablets. In 540 B.C. Pisistratus endowed Athens with the first public library.

book manufacturing The process of composition, printing and binding of a book.

book paper Paper produced principally for use in the printing of booklets, books and magazines.

book review Critical accounts of books published in newspapers and magazines.

bookseller A business that specializes in the retail sale of books.

Books in Print A reference and acquisition tool for librarians and booksellers. Books in Print is a multivolum set of books that lists book titles that are currently available from publishers.

bookstore The bookstore was born in London with the bookstore of Wynkyn de Worde, successor to William Caxton, and publisher of the first book to be produced in English in Great Britain, in 1495. But it was not until the late 16th century that bookshops began to specialize in selling books from one field or another, and it was only then that publishers charged them with the task of distrubuting their products.

boot To start up a computer. Microcomputers have a bootstrap routine in a ROM chip that is automatically executed when the computer is turned on or reset. It searches for the operating system, loads it and then passes control over to it.

border A rule or linear design that encloses an element of a layout, such as a block of type or graphic. Used to set off the enclosed element from the rest of the page. A border should complement or harmonize with the material it surrounds.

border

border structure A basic design style with the elements enclosed in a frame or border.

bounce Alternating characters in an up and down position.

bounce

bowl The enclosed oval or round curve of letters like "D,", "R," "O," "e," and "b."

box A rectangular frame of ruled lines around type matter or illustrations. Also text or images isolated by a rectangular screen.

boxhead The heading at the top of a column in a list or table.

bracket A symbol usually used to enclose supplementary text, [ ].

bracketed This term describes the linking of the main stem of a character (vertical) to the serif (horizontal).

break An interruption in the flow of text between paragraphs. See *page break*.

brilliant   Tiny 3.5 point type.

broadsheet   A term commonly used to refer to a page the size of a full-size newspaper.

broadside   (1) A term used for any printed piece on an oversized sheet; a poster-sized publication. (2) A page designed to be read normally when the book is rotated 90 degrees; landscape page.

brownout   An extended period of insufficient power line voltage. It can damage computer equipment.

browse   To view information without manipulating it.

brush   Typefaces which appear to have been drawn with a brush or broad pointed pen. A casual or informal feeling results from the use of "brush" faces.

buffer   (1) A holding area for data. (2) Main or available memory in a computer or laser printer, used for storing fonts to be used, documents being printed, images, routines or data in use.

bug   A flaw in the design or implementation of a software program or hardware design which causes erroneous results or malfunctions.

built-in font   A printer font encoded permanently in the read-only memory (ROM) of a PostScript printer.

bulk   The thickness of paper. See *pages per inch*.

bullet   Solid dot used as an ornamental character or to set off items in lists.

bullet

business graphics   (1) Pie charts, bar charts, scattergrams, graphs, and other visual representations of the operational or strategic aspects of a business, such as sales vs. costs, sales by department, comparative product performance, and stock prices. (2) Applications programs that allow the user to display data as visual presentations. (3) With the advent of low-cost computers, graphics packages are now available for creating business graphics where virtually any type of data set can be displayed as graphs, charts, and histograms.

business graphics

bus network One of the three principal topologies for a local area network, in which all stations, or computer devices, communicate by using a common distribution channel, or bus. See *network, ring network* and *star network*.

button The button on a mouse.

byline A credit line telling the reader who wrote an article.

byte Eight binary bits of data grouped together to represent a character, digit or other value. A common unit of computer storage from personal computers to mainframe computers.

c & lc Abbreviation for Caps and Lower Case, a style of composition in which the first letter of each word starts with a capital. A proofreader's mark.

c & sc Abbreviation for Caps and Small Caps, a style where words begin with a capital letter and have the remaining letters in small capitals which are the same height as the body of lower case letters. A proofreader's mark for caps and small caps.

cache A faster memory in which parts of the information in the main (slower) memory or disk are copied. Information that is likely to require reading or alteration goes to the cache, where the system can access it more quickly. Caching can significantly speed processing of some programs, especially if floppy disks are used for mass storage.

caliper The thickness of paper in thousandths of an inch.

calligraphic In typography, this usually refers to Roman or Italic alphabets which appear to have been written with a pen or brush. Derived from the Greek word "kalligraphia," which means "beautiful writing." The "chancery" script of the 15th Century became the model for *italics*.

calligraphic

callouts Arrows or other graphic elements used to call attention to and explain the parts of a diagram, illustration or picture.

camera ready copy Art or copy that is ready for printing, occupying, silk-screening or whatever reproduction method is in force. Camera ready pages with art are called mechanicals.

cancel (1) Keyboard operation that deletes the line currently being typed. (2) To end a task before it is completed.

canned software Programs prepared by computer manufacturers or software developers and provided to a user in ready-to-use form. General enough to be used by many businesses and individuals. Contrast with *custom software*.

canned text Alternate term for boilerplate.

canopy A headline that runs across picture and horizontally adjacent story.

cap A contraction of capital, meaning an upper case character.

capacity Number of items of data that a storage device is capable of containing. Frequently defined in terms of computer words, bytes, or characters.

cap height Height of a capital letter measured from baseline to the top of the character.

cap line The imaginary line which represents the uppermost part of capital letters and some character's ascenders. The distance from the cap line to the baseline is called the cap height.

Tampa, Florida

cap line

caps Capital letters. All caps means that all letters are capitalized; initial caps means the capitalization of the first letter of each significant word. ALL CAPS WOULD LOOK LIKE THIS.

caption Explanatory text that accompanies illustrations, tables or photographs. Often they are set in a different style of type than the body text.

card An arrangement of text and graphics intended to sell a product or service. Also called an "advertisement."

carding The insertion of very small amounts of additional space between lines of type, generally to assist in vertical justification.

carpel-tunnel syndrome A type of repetitive stress injury that affects the wrist. Repeated and prolonged typing at a keyboard can cause this serious disorder.

carriage return (CR) In a printer the operation that causes the next character to be printed at the left margin.

carry forward Instruction to transfer text to the next column or page.

carryover Text that continues beyond its initial column or page.

cartography Art and science of making maps.

cartoon Humorous drawing in a book, magazine, newspaper or some other publication.

cartridge A generic term that can refer to any of several devices that are self-contained, usually in some kind of plastic housing. For example, ROM cartridge, disk cartridge, toner cartridge, memory cartridge, tape cartridge, or font cartridge.

case The cover of a book inside which the binder's boards are placed and glued.

casebound A hardcover book.

casting off Calculating the number of words or character in a manuscript in order to estimate its typeset length. The purpose is both to calculate the quantity of paper needed and to estimate the probable cost of production.

catalog A systematic list of books or other items in a collection or group of collections.

Cataloging in Publication (CIP) The purpose of the Cataloging in Publication (CIP) program is to prepare prepublication cataloging records for those books most likely to be widely acquired by the nation's libraries. These records (CIP data) are printed in the book and greatly facilitate cataloging activities for libraries. They are also distributed prior to the book's publication in machine readable form, alerting libraries and other bibliographic services around the world to forthcoming titles. The CIP program began in 1971 and is supported by the Library of Congress.

catchline A line of display type between a photograph and its caption.

cathode ray tube (CRT) Electronic tube with a screen upon which information may be displayed.

CD-ROM An acronym for compact disk read-only memory, a type of optical disk that uses the same basic technology as do the popular CD audio disks. Although a CD-ROM drive can only read data (the data is permanently stamped onto the disks during manufacturing), the disks are inexpensive to make and can each hold about 650 megabytes of data. Contents are typically an entire encyclopedia on a single CD, a set of reference works, a clip-art library, a collection of fine art, or any other publication which is for reading only.

center align To line up text in the middle of a page or column.

centered Text that aligns centered along an imaginary vertical line between the left and right margins.

centered

centerline Imaginary vertical line through the middle of a page. The centerline is used to align type and visual elements on the page.

center spread Two facing pages at the center of a brochure, magazine or newspaper.

central processing unit (CPU) A microprocessor that contains the sequencing and processing facilities for instruction execution, timing functions, initial program loading, and other machine-related functions. The computing part of the computer.

CGA Acronym for Color Graphics Adapter. The original low-resolution color standard for IBM PC's. CGA has been superseded by EGA and VGA.

chapbook Small, inexpensive book or pamphlet of poems, short stories, essays, ballads or folk tales.

chapter A major division of a book.

chapter opener The first page of each chapter in a book; usually designed separately from other chapter pages.

character Single typographic element including letters, numerals and punctuation marks.

character attribute A character emphasis, such as boldface and italic, or the size and font of the type.

character count Number of letters and spaces in a headline of a given width.

character recognition Technology of using machines to identify human-readable symbols automatically, and then to express their identities in machine-readable codes. This operation of transforming numbers and letters into a form directly suitable for data processing is an important method of introducing information into computing systems.

characters per inch (cpi) Method of expression for the output from printers as determined by type size and style.

characters per pica (cpp) The average number of characters in a specific point size and typeface that will fit in 1 pica of horizontal space. Used in copyfitting calculations.

characters per second (cps) Unit for measuring output of low-speed serial printers.

chart

chart Visual representation of quantitative information — such as a bar graph, in which the information is made visual by heavy horizontal or vertical lines, or a circle graph or pie chart, in which the information is pictured as slices of an imaginary pie.

checking draft A draft upon which corrections and changes are marked.

chimney A series of heads or pictures of the same width stacked to fill an entire column or set of columns on a page.

chip A miniaturized electronic circuit. They hold from a few dozen to several million electronic components (transistors, resistors, etc.).

Christian Booksellers Association (CBA) A trade organization of religious bookstores and suppliers.

Cicero European equivalent of the pica, but fractionally larger. Used as a unit for measuring the width or measure of a line of type and the depth of a page. One Cicero = 4.511 mm = 12 Didot points = 12.835 points. See *Didot*.

CIP Acronym for Cataloging In Publication, a program designed to prepare prepublication cataloging records for books most likely to be widely acquired by the nation's libraries. These records are printed in the book and greatly facilitate cataloging activities for libraries.

circuit board Thin insulating board used to mount and connect various electronic components and microchips in a pattern of conductive lines. This circuit pattern is etched into the board's surface.

circus makeup A wild, jumbled page layout.

clarendon A typeface with squared-off serifs.

clay coated paper Paper that has been coated with clay particles during manufacturing and finished to a smooth surface. Clay coated papers are ideally suited for use in laser printers.

clean copy Manuscript copy with few errors.

clean up To remove typographical errors from a manuscript.

clear (1) Keyboard function that removes the contents from the display screen. (2) Same as zap.

click Means to point the mouse pointer at a word or icon on the screen, press the mouse button, and then release it quickly. Clicking is usually performed to select or deselect an item or to activate a program or program feature.

client Any computer using the services of a computer network.

client/server system A computer system in which personal computers or workstations function as "clients" that request services from print servers, file servers, database servers, etc., which may be located at remote sites.

clip To select a part of a graphic to show on the screen or place into a document. Clipping is used to select a region of interest rather than scaling the entire image.

clip art Collections of pictures and design elements (such as borders, symbols, drawings, etc.). The collections may be in printed form or stored on diskettes or CD-ROM. This pre-drawn artwork can be used in designing newsletters, brochures, flyers, books, magazines and incorporated into other documents.

clip art

clipboard A temporary holding place that facilitates the cutting and pasting of text and graphics. Clipboard information is held in memory only while the computer is turned on. A clipboard allows information to be transferred from one program to another. A clipboard stores a copy of the last information that was "copied" or "cut." A "paste" operation passes data from the clipboard to the current program.

clock speed The internal heartbeat of a computer, governing the speed of the processor. For example, the same processor running at 40 megahertz (million cycles per second) is twice as fast internally as one running at 20 megahertz.

clone Technically, a clone is an identical copy of some device. With regard to computers, a clone is a compatible computer that is capable of running the same software as the original machine. It also implies the machine can use similar components as the original, although this is not always true.

close To finish and save.

close box A small square in the upper-left corner of the window. Clicking this box closes the active window.

closed A character or symbol that is essentially "filled in" or solid; the opposite of open, which describes a character or symbol that exists as an outline.

CLOSED  OPEN

closed

close set type Type which has the same leading value as its point size — 11/11, 10/10, etc.

cloth Material used for making casebound book covers.

CMYK Acronym for Cyan, Magenta, Yellow and Black, the colors used in 4-color process printing. They are not primary colors, but secondary colors derived from mixing primary additive colors: red, green and blue.

co-author Person who participates with another in the creation of a work.

coffee table book A large art book with lavish color illustrations and photographs.

coated paper Paper that is treated with clay or some other pigmented material to make a smoother printing surface. Used in books with high-quality illustrations.

coin-edge Broken rule border composed of small, parallel vertical lines resembling milling on the edge of a coin.

cold boot A computer start-up that begins when the power is turned on.

collate Gathering of document pages in a specified order.

colophon (1) A paragraph in the back of a book describing the typeface used, its designer, its history, and other production aspects of the book. (2) A logo that identifies a publisher. (3) A Greek term meaning "finishing touch."

color correction (1) Adjustment of component colors in photographic or digital images to alter or enhance the image, compensate for printing, etc. (2) Adjusting color levels of a bit mapped image by using a paint program.

color graphics Any type of computer graphic in which the images displayed on a visual display screen, printed copy, or other type of display are shown in more than one color.

color graphics adapter (CGA) An adapter that simultaneously provides four colors. It allows a computer to show color graphics as well as text.

color key A set of four color-acetate overlays based on color separation halftones and used as a pre-press proof.

color monitor A computer display designed to work with a video card or adapter to produce text or graphics image in color. A color monitor has a screen coated internally with three phosphors — one each for red, green and blue. To light the phosphor and produce a spot of color, such a monitor also usually contains three electron guns — again, one for each of the three colors.

color overlay A page that includes one color to be used in your publication. A separate page is printed for each color. All graphics and text to be printed in one particular color are located in their proper positions on the page.

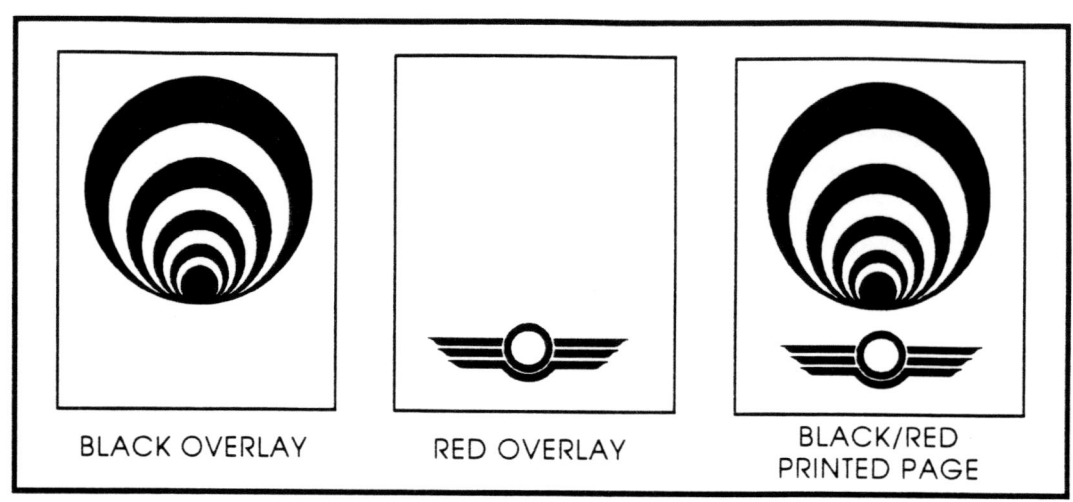

color overlay

color resolution The number of different colors or gray-scale values a system can produce or work with. A value is usually given in bits.

color separation The creation of a multicolored graphic by creating several layers, with each layer corresponding to one of the colors that will be printed when the graphic is reproduced by a commercial printer. See *CMYK* and *four color process printing*.

column guides The dotted, vertical, nonprinting lines that mark the left and right edges of columns — used to help position elements on a page.

column inch An area that is 1 inch deep by 1 column wide.

column rule A vertical division line that runs between columns of type.

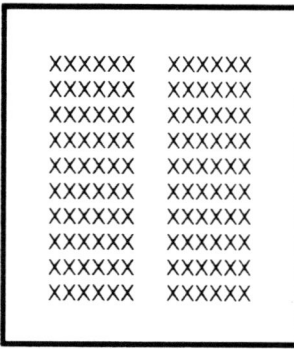

column width

column width Horizontal measurement of typeset lines. Also line length and measure.

columns Vertical arrangements of text on a page.

comb binding A method of binding in which plastic teeth fit through notches in the pages. Also called *plastic binding*.

comb binding

COMDEX An acronym for COMputer Dealer's EXposition, the largest computer trade show in the world. Held in the United States and in other locations throughout the world.

comic book A book or booklet using cartoons to tell a story.

Committee of Small Magazines, Editors, and Publishers A national trade association for small publishers. See *COSMEP*.

comp Abbreviation for comprehensive. An accurate representation of a finished printed piece showing type and illustrations in position on the page.

COMP Acronym for COMPosite artwork, a layout for presentation purposes. Also called COMPrehensive artwork.

compatible Refers to two machines capable of using the same software as well as the same hardware components.

complimentary copy A free copy of a book or other publication.

composite character A new character that is made up of two or more characters already existing in the font.

composition Material (type and art) designed on a desktop publishing system or by hand. Also involves typesetting and arranging it into pages. Broadly speaking, composition is equivalent to typesetting.

compositor A person who sets type.

compress To save storage space by eliminating gaps, empty fields, redundancy or unnecessary data to shorten the length of records or files.

computer

computer Device capable of solving problems or manipulating data by accepting data, performing prescribed operations (mathematical or logical) on the data, and supplying the results of these operations.

computer accessories The equipment that can be attached to a computer, such as mouse, disk drive, visual display device, keyboard, or printer.

computer center Facility that provides computer services to a variety of users through the operation of computer and auxiliary hardware, and through ancillary services provided by its staff.

computer classifications Digital computers are broken down into three classifications: mainframes (which includes supercomputers), minicomputers and microcomputers.

computerese Jargon and other specialized vocabulary of people working with computers and information processing systems.

computer family A term commonly used to indicate a group of computers that are built around the same microprocessor, or around a series of related microprocessors and that share significant design features. For example, the IBM PC and IBM PS/2 models represent a family designed by IBM Corporation around the Intel 80x86 series of microprocessors (80286, 80386 and 80486).

computer graphics General term meaning the appearance of pictures or diagrams, as distinct from letters and numbers, on the display screen or hard-copy output device. The term computer graphics encompasses different methods of generating, displaying, and storing information.

computer graphics

computer graphics artist A person who uses computers as tools in producing commercial art and fine art.

computerize To automate by means of computer systems.

computer jargon Technical vocabulary associated with the computer field.

computer network An interconnected complex of two or more computer systems.

computer program A specific set of software commands in a form acceptable to a computer and used to achieve a desired result.

computer publishing Refers to the design and production of printed matter using computer equipment.

computer resource Any of the computer system elements needed to perform required operations, including software, data files, processing units, input-output units, storage units and operating personnel.

computer security Preservation of computing resources against abuse or unauthorized use, especially the protection of data from accidental or deliberate damage, disclosure, or modification.

computer store Retail store where customers can select, from the shelf or the floor, a full computer system or just a few accessories. These stores typically sell software, books, supplies, and periodicals. In a broad-based computer store, one can examine and operate several types of microcomputer systems.

computer system System that includes computer hardware, software, and people. Used to process data into useful information.

computer user Any person who uses a computer system or its output.

computer users group Group whose members share the knowledge they have gained and the programs they have developed on a computer or class of computers of a certain manufacturer. Most groups hold meetings and distribute newsletters to exchange information, trade equipment, and share computer programs.

computer vendor Organization that manufactures, sells, or services computer equipment.

computer virus A program that attaches itself to other programs or data. A virus' typical purpose is to disrupt the processing of information on an infected system. When an infected program is executed, the virus reproduces and spreads by searching for other software that is not infected, and then attaching itself to previously "clean" software.

computing power The relative speed of computing. One computer is described as being more powerful than another if it can handle more work at a faster speed.

ABCDEFGHIJKLMNOPQRSTUVWXYZ
abcdefghijklmnopqrstuvwxyz
1234567890&?!$(.,;:)

condensed type

condensed type Type narrowed in width so that more characters will fit into a linear inch. Narrow version of a typeface.

C1S Abbreviation for Coated One Side, a popular book cover paper that has been coated on one side only.

configuration (1) A particular arrangement of computer equipment including a computer, peripherals, and interfaces, all of which will work efficiently together. (2) Layout or design of elements in a hardware or computer graphics system.

consignment   The placing of books in a bookstore in which the publisher is paid only upon the sale of the books.

continuous   Adjacent or adjoining.

continuation line   That which indicates that a story or article is continued from a previous page.

continuous forms   Fanfold paper or roll paper that has small holes on the outer edges for automatic feeding into printers. Can be blank sheets or preprinted forms.

continuous tone   An image made up of a wide range of actual colors or tones from black to white, not broken up into dots and not restricted by a specified grid. Photographs are continuous tones, computer screen images and bit map images are constructed of same-size picture elements of pixels.

contour   (1) To set type so as to wrap-around an illustration or other non-text element on a page. (2) A photograph from which all the background has been removed.

contoured text   Text whose letters have been lowered, raised, flipped, or otherwise manipulated to present some overall graphic impression.

contrast   (1) An indication of the difference between the thicker and thinner parts of characters in a typeface. Times, with its thin serifs and horizontal strokes and thick verticals, is a high contrast face. Avant Garde is a low contrast face. (2) The difference between the light and dark gray areas of an image. The higher the contrast the fewer shades of gray between black and white.

contrast

control key   Special-function key on a computer keyboard. Used simultaneously with another key to enter a command instructing the system to perform a task.

controller Within the computer, the controller is a hardware device that controls the activities of peripheral devices such as a disk drive or display terminal.

co-op publishing Two or more individuals or publishers join forces to publish a book.

copier paper Smooth, white, 20 lb. weight paper made for general use in photocopy machines and laser printers.

copperplate A typeface that does not usually has a lowercase, using smaller point size caps in place of them. Used primarily for business cards or business stationery.

coprocessor A device that performs specialized processing in conjunction with the main microprocessor of a system. It works in tandem with another central processing unit to increase the computing power of a system. An extra microprocessor to handle some things faster than the main processor, i.e., a math coprocessor or a graphics coprocessor.

copy (1) To reproduce data in a new location or other destination, leaving the source data unchanged, although the physical form of the result may differ from that of the source; for example, to make a duplicate of all the programs or data on a disk. (2) To copy a graphic screen image to a printer. (3) Any material to be printed.

copyedit To edit a piece of copy (e.g., a manuscript) before it is set in type. Not to be confused with "proofread" which refers specifically to the checking of typeset proofs.

copyfitting (1) Mathematically determining the area that a given amount of typewritten copy will occupy when set in type. (2) Editing written material and adjusting typography for the purpose of making the text fit a layout. (3) The process of turning a manuscript into a rough book format to determine how long the finished book will be.

copy protection Methods used by software developers to prevent any copying of their programs. To protect against illegal copying of software, many software developers build copy protection routines into their programs. Copy protection techniques are sometimes sophisticated, although several commercial programs exist that allow users to override many standard copy-protection techniques.

copyright (1) Recognized ownership of creative work; protection against unauthorized use of work. (2) In book typography, commonly on the back of the title page, a left-hand page (verso).

copyright infringement The unauthorized use of copyrighted material.

copyright notice Statement of copyright ownership that has three elements: the symbol © and/or word "copyright," the year of publication, and the name of the copyright owner. For example, "Copyright © 1996 by John Smith."

copyright page The page in the frontmatter of a book that contains the copyright notice.

corrupted file A file with distorted data.

COSMEP Acronym for Committee Of Small Magazines, Editors, and Publishers. COSMEP is a national trade association for small publishers. The association holds an annual conference, issues a monthly newsletter, exhibits members publications at international conventions and performs other services for members.

counter The enclosed (or partially enclosed) space within letters such as "c," "e," "s," "H," and "g." Counter refers to the "space," where the term "bowl" refers to the lines enclosing the counter.

Courier A standard monospace typeface commonly found on typewriters.

cover stock In printing, paper used for the covers of catalogs, reports, books, and other publications. It is slightly thicker than paper used for book pages.

cpi See *characters per inch.*

cps See *characters per second.*

cpu See *central processing unit.*

crash (1) An unplanned program termination due to a hardware or software failure. (2) Sudden failure of a program or a disk drive, usually causing the loss of data. See *bomb*.

crease Alternate term for *score*.

creative designer The individual who lays out and designs a page.

credit line Name of artist, illustrator or photographer for a graphic element or picture..

crop To trim a graphics image for a better fit or to eliminate unwanted portions. In preparing an illustration for traditional printing, cropping is used to clean up a graphic for placement in a document.

crop

crop marks Intersecting lines that mark the corners of a page and define its actual or trimmed size.

crop marks

crossbar A horizontal stroke that crosses through the stem, such as in the lowercase t.

crossfooting A check on the accuracy of figures in a table: find the total across each row and the total of each column. The sum of all the row totals and the sum of all the column totals should be the same.

crosshair cursor A digitizing device that is often moved over hard-copy images of maps and drawings to enter those images into the computer system.

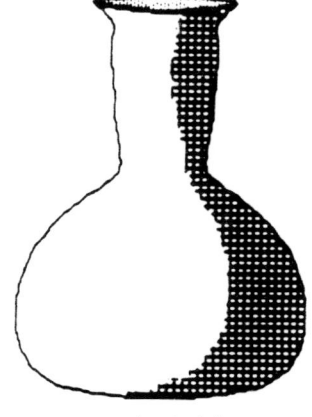

crosshair cursor

crosshatching In computer graphics, the shading of some portion of a drawing with a pattern of intersecting lines or figures repeated across the area being shaded. Crosshatching is one of several methods for filling in areas of a graphic.

crosshatching

cross stroke The part of the letter that cuts horizontally across the stem, like in the letters "t" and "f."

crotch The inside of an apex or vortex. See *apex*.

CRT Acronym for Cathode Ray Tube, the picture tube of the standard computer display screen. A CRT display is built around a vacuum tube containing one or more electron guns whose electron beams rapidly sweep horizontally across the inside of the front surface of the tube, which is coated with a material that glows when irradiated.

current directory The directory that an operating system or application program uses by default to store and retrieve files.

current drive The disk drive currently being used by the computer system.

current font The most recently selected typeface and type size.

current page box An area that displays the current page being worked on.

cursive First used in the 16th century, these typefaces imitate handwriting. Script letters and cursive typefaces appear to be drawn with pen and ink. Unlike script, however, cursive letters are not joined.

cursor (1) Moving, sliding, or blinking symbol on a CRT screen that indicates where the next character will appear. (2) Position indicator used on a video display terminal to indicate a character to be connected or a position in which data is to be entered. (3) On graphic systems, it can take any shape (arrow, square, paintbrush, etc.) and is used to mark where the next graphic action is to take place.

custom page size A nonstandard page size.

custom software Software designed and programmed for a customer, in contrast with software that is available off the shelf for a particular use such as accounting, graphics or desktop publishing.

cut Act of removing text or graphics from a document.

cut and paste Method employed by some systems to move graphics and/or text from one location to another. Such systems usually permit the performance of other operations between the cut and the paste steps. Cut and paste enables compatible programs to store text and graphics.

cutline The newspaper term for a caption.

cutout (1) A graphic element separated from its background for use in assembling an image. (2) A specific shape cut out of the printed sheet with a specially made steel die.

cut sheets Individual pieces of paper, laser printers generally use stacks of cut sheets.

cyrillic Refers to language and alphabets common to Russia, Czechoslovakia, Yugoslavia and Turkey.

dagger A symbol used as a reference mark in footnoting.

daisywheel printer Printer that uses a metal or plastic disk with printed characters along its edge. The disk rotates until the required character is brought before a hammer that strikes it against a ribbon.

dash (1) Punctuation mark. (2) Small horizontal rule used as decoration. In typesetting, the dash family includes the hyphen, the en dash, and the em dash in order of size.

data Formalized representation of facts or concepts suitable for communication, interpretation, or processing by people or by automatic means. Raw material of information. Individual pieces of quantitative information, such as dollar sales of carpets, numbers of building permits issued, units of raw material on hand. Historically, data is a plural noun while datum is singular — a distinction now generally ignored in data processing terminology.

database A set of interrelated files that is created and managed by a database management system.

database management system (DBMS) Collection of hardware and software that organizes and provides access to a database. The computer program provides the mechanisms needed to create a computerized database file, to add data to the file, to alter data in the file, to organize data within the file, to search for data in the file, and so forth. In other words, it manages data.

data compression Technique that saves computer storage space by eliminating empty fields, gap redundancies, or unnecessary data to reduce the size of the length of records.

data entry Process of entering data directly into a computer system.

data file A collection of data records.

dead matter (1) Material that is no longer needed; superfluous verbiage in a manuscript. Also called "deadwood." (2) Useless information in computer files.

dealer One who sells for profit computer-related equipment, software, and services.

debossing Printing process in which an area of the paper is recessed.

debug To detect, locate, and remove all mistakes in a computer program and any malfunctions in the computing system itself.

decorative rule Printing element that produces horizontal dividers that are more ornate in form than a simple line or lines.

dedicated Pertaining to programs, machines, or procedures that are designed or reserved for special use.

dedication page In book typography, a new right-hand (recto) page or may be on the back of the title page. This is the page on which the author dedicates his or her work.

de facto standard A programming language, hardware product, design or program that has become so widely used and imitated that it has little competition but those whose status has not officially been declared by a recognized standard establishing organization.

default Assumption made by a system or program when no specific choice is given by the program or the user. A choice that has been pre-set for you. You can override it or simply accept the setting which the manufacturer or developer has deemed most likely appropriate.

defragmentation A process in which all the files on a hard disk are rewritten so that all parts of each file are written to contiguous sectors. The reorganization of a file to eliminate fragmentation.

delete To remove or eliminate. Eliminating a defined portion of text. To erase data from a file.

delete key A keyboard key that erases the character above or to the right of the on-screen cursor.

delimiter Special character, often a comma or space, used to separate variable names of items in a list or to separate one string of characters from another, as in the separation of data items.

demand printing Where only enough copies are printed to meet the immediate market demand.

density Number of characters that can be stored in a given physical space. Measures how close together data are recorded on a magnetic medium, usually in bytes per inch. As recording density increases, the capacity of a storage device increases. See *double density*.

descender Portion of lower-case letters (g, j, p, q, and y) that extends below the baseline of other characters.

descender

descender line The lowest line that a character's descender extends to, like the bottom stem of the lowercase "j" and "y."

descent A font's maximum distance below the baseline.

desk accessory (DA) In a graphical user interface, helpful utilities (e.g., calculator, notepad, thesaurus, paint program, word processor, etc.) that you can open when you are in the middle of any program. Desk accessories are accessed by selecting them from a special pull-down menu. Desk accessories are conveniences that can be activated when needed and then either put away or moved to a small part of the display screen.

desktop (1) Screen display containing icons that represent programs, files or resources available to the user. (2) Small enough to fit on the top of an office desk, particularly a computer system.

desktop computer A computer that will fit on the top of a standard size office desk. Most personal computers and lap computers can be considered desktop computers. A desktop computer is equipped with sufficient internal memory and auxiliary storage to perform business computing tasks.

desktop publishing (dtp) When printed pieces including words and pictures (ads, newsletters, magazines, brochures, books) are created almost entirely on a computer. Desktop publishing programs convert normal text into

desktop computer

professional quality documents that can be printed on laser printers or imagesetters. The term "desktop publishing" was coined by Paul Brainerd, president of Aldus Corporation, the developer of PageMaker.

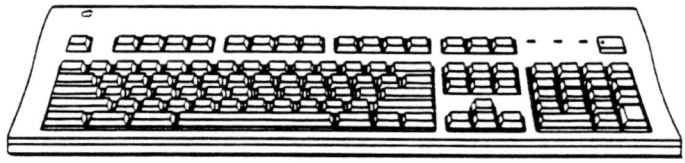
detachable keyboard

detachable keyboard Keyboard not built into the same case as the video display or desk unit. Connects to the system with a cable and allows greater flexibility in positioning of the keyboard display — one result of *ergonomics*.

device driver A special section of computer code that translates the general commands from an operating system or user programs into the exact code a specific peripheral device needs. Often, device drivers for a few standard peripherals are built into the operating system, but others must be added in installation. For example: your printer needs a driver, your mouse needs a driver. Generally speaking, drivers come with the new hardware or as part of any major software package. Once installed, you can forget about them.

diacritic A mark, like a circumflex, accent mark, cedilla, or umlaut, which is added to a letter to give it a special phonetic value, or to distinguish words which are otherwise graphically identical. Also called "accent."

diagnostic (1) A message sent to the user by the computer system pinpointing errors in syntax or logic. (2) Diagnostics are often referred to as error messages.

dialog box Interactive message box. A temporary window on the screen that contains a set of choices whenever the executing program needs to collect information from the user.

dictionaries Reference books. A dictionary is an alphabetical list of words or names, with definitions. The oldest dictionary to have been found dates back to 600 B.C. It comes from Mesopotamia and is written in Akkadian, the language of the Assyrians and the Babylonians. In China, the Hou Chin dictionary did not appear until 150 B.C. In 1480 the printer William Caxton (Great Britain) published the first bilingual English-French dictionary for tourists. It had 36 pages. In 1755 the English lexicographer, Samuel Johnson (1709-1784), produced *A Dictionary of the English Language*.

Didot The base unit of measure in the Didot or French Point System of type measure. The Didot system of measuring type size is based on the French inch. 12 Didot points = 1 Cicero = 4.511 mm = 12.835 points. Named after Francoise Didot, its inventor. See *Cicero*.

die cut In printing, the process of cutting designs into paper.

die stamping The imprinting of lettering or a design on a book cover.

differential spacing See *proportional spacing*.

diffusion A special effects filtering method that randomly distributes gray levels in a pattern that achieves a mezzotint effect.

digital computer A computer that operates on discrete data. A device that performs arithmetic, logical, and comparative functions upon information represented in digital form and that operates under control of an internal program. Digital means that the computer uses data in the form of discrete numbers; for example, binary ones and zeros. Most computers used today (mainframes, minicomputers and microcomputers), are digital.

digital photography A special camera known as a digitizer takes electronic pictures which are translatable onto a computer monitor in the form of dots. Your eyes see the pixels as a pattern similar to the screen dot pattern of a newspaper photo when viewed with a magnifying glass. A digitized picture is created from these tiny pixels the way a wall mural's thousands of ceramic tiles combine to make a complete picture. The pixels can be manipulated as though they were the tiles of a mural. The resultant imagery only looks like a photograph. It is really an assemblage of pixels. Also called "pixel photography" and "pixelgraphy."

digital press In April 1992 a new digital printing press, the Electrobook Press, was unveiled. It was developed by a partnership of three companies: press manufacturer AM International Inc.; printer R.R. Donnelly & Sons; and publisher McGraw-Hill. The press operates using digital electronic imaging and electrophotographic printing. Dubbed "electronic imaging," the system does not require printing plates and can print two sides of the paper simultaneously. The press is designed to primarily produce books.

digital type Type fonts stored in a form readable by computers. Digitized type is broken up as a series of dots or vertical lines.

digitize (1) To register a visual image or real object in a format that can be processed by the computer. Digitized data are read into the system with graphics input devices. It includes scanning an image, tracing a picture on a graphics tablet or converting camera images into the computer. (2) To convert an analog signal (voltage or temperature) into a digital value.

digitizing Process of converting graphic representations, such as pictures and drawings, into digital data that can be processed by a computer system.

digitizing camera A camera coupled with a processor used for encoding highly detailed images such as pictures or three-dimensional objects into digital data.

digitizing tablet

digitizing tablet A graphic input device that allows the user to create images. It has a special stylus that can be used to draw or trace images, which are then converted to digital data that can be processed by the computer.

dimmed command A command in a pull-down menu that is grayed-black. A dimmed command means that choice is not currently available to you; perhaps because another function needs to be accomplished before that selection can be made.

dimmed icon A grayed-black icon indicates that the object it represents, such as a disk, or a folder, or document on a disk, has either been opened or been ejected from the disk drive.

dingbats Small graphical elements used for decorative purposes in a document. Some fonts, such as Zapf Dingbats, are designed to present sets of dingbats. Entire typefaces of dingbats are sometimes referred to as pi fonts.

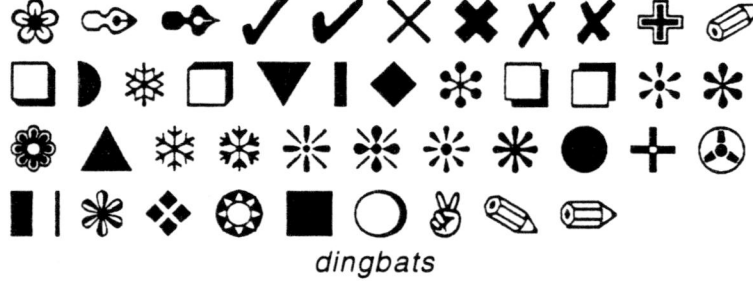
dingbats

diphthong Two vowels joined to form a single character.

directory (1) In a partition by software into several distinct files, a directory is maintained on a device to locate these files. (2) Index file containing the names and locations of all the files contained on a storage medium. (3) Major section of your hard disk drive. You can name as many directories as you like, and create subdirectories within them. As you create files, then, you will store the files in the directories. (4) Publication giving names, addresses, and phone numbers. The first city directory was for the city and suburbs of Philadelphia. It was published by John Macpherson in 1785 and it included 6,250 names and addresses.

direct positive Photostat made without an intermediate paper negative.

dirty copy Copy unsuitable for reproduction, as compared to *clean copy*.

disclaimer Clause associated with many software products that states the vendor is not responsible for any business losses incurred due to the use of the product.

discretionary hyphen A special character placed in word processing files that shows where a word may be broken. Sometimes called a "ghost hyphen."

disk Magnetic device for storing information and programs accessible by a computer. Can be either a rigid platter (*hard disk*) or a sheet of flexible plastic (*floppy disk*). Disks have tracks where data is stored.

disk cache An area of computer memory where data is temporarily stored on its way to or from a disk.

disk capacity The storage capacity of a hard or floppy disk, usually in kilobytes (KB), megabytes (MB), or gigabytes (GB).

disk crash Condition of a disk unit that makes it unusable. Usually caused by contact between the read/write head of the disk drive and the surface of the disk.

disk directory A catalog. This is the computer's own record of where each file or program is stored on the disk. The directory usually takes up a few tracks at the beginning of a disk.

disk drive Device that reads data from a magnetic disk and copies it into the computer's memory so it can be used by the computer, and that writes data from the computer's memory onto a disk so it can be stored. See *floppy disk* and *hard disk*.

diskette A single magnetic disk on which data is recorded as magnetic spots. Available in both 3.5-inch format and 5.25-inch format.

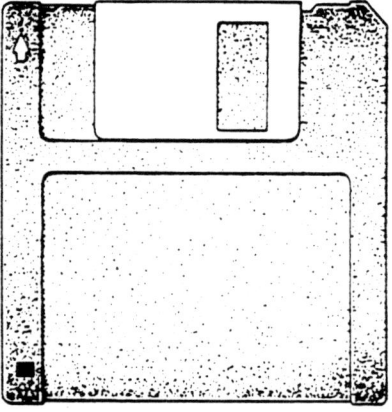

diskette

disk operating system (DOS) A collection of software stored on disk that controls the operation of the computer system. A computer cannot function unless it has access to its own operating system. Typically, it keeps track of files, saves and retrieves files, allocates storage space, and manages other control functions associated with disk storage.

display

display (1) Physical representation of data, as on a screen or display. (2) Lights or indicators on computer consoles. (3) Process of creating a visual representative of graphic data on an output device. (4) Arrangement of typographic elements to make them conspicuous and appealing to the reader. (5) The sizes of type used for headlines.

display type Type that is larger than the text type of a document — typically 18 points or greater. Also refers to certain styles of typefaces that are more appropriate for display rather than body text.

display type

distortion Altering the height-to-width ratio of a picture when resizing it.

distributor A business that represents publishers and sells their books to bookstores and libraries.

dithering Creating levels of gray on either a laser printer or a computer screen by combining the basic pixels or raster dots into larger sized dots giving the perception of a shade of gray from a distance. Dithering can also be used to create an image closely resembling a halftone. See h*alftone*.

divider A breaker subhead, usually of 14 points or larger.

document (1) A file containing text or drawing to be printed. (2) A printed form containing text and/or illustrations.

document publishing The prepress production of lengthy documents such as textbooks, scientific reports, manuals, etc.

document reader An input device that reads printed data into a computer system. The data is interpreted by an optical character recognition program as text.

dogleg A column extending from what is otherwise a rectangular area of body type.

DOS Operating system for IBM-compatible microcomputers. DOS is available in both generic MS-DOS and IBM-specific PC DOS versions. DOS is an acronym for *Disk Operating System.*

dot A pixel. See *pixel*.

dot gain A printing situation where halftone dots print larger than they should making the region darker.

dot matrix printer Printer that creates text characters and graphs with a series of closely spaced dots. Uses tiny hammers to strike a needle mechanism against the paper at precise moments as the print head moves across the page. Some produce dot patterns fine enough to approach the print quality of an electric typewriter. See *laser printer*.

dots per inch (1) A linear measure of the number of dots a printer can print in an inch. For example, a 600 dpi laser printer can print up to 600 dots for each horizontal or vertical inch on the paper. (2) A measure of screen resolution that counts the dots that the device can produce per linear inch.

double-click Method to invoke a command by using the mouse button. The pointer or cursor is placed in the correct position on a display screen and the mouse button is pressed twice in rapid succession. A double-click is used to open a file, disk, or folder.

double column Two columns side by side.

double density Having twice the storage capacity of a normal disk or tape. Ability to store twice as much data in a given area on a disk or tape as *single density*.

double numeration In book design, a notation system in which sections of text and illustrations are designated by a chapter number and a serial number.

double-page spread Two facing pages which are treated as one in terms of design. Facing pages may share a single illustration.

double-sided disk Magnetic disk capable of storing information on both of its surfaces. See *floppy disk*.

double sided pages The pages in a publication that will be reproduced on both sides of a sheet of paper.

double space type Type set with one blank line of space between each two lines of type.

double truck The center page spread of a publication; two pages that are locked together and printed on the same piece of paper.

download (1) Process of transferring data (files) from a large computer to a smaller one. (2) To transfer information to a laser printer from a computer. Opposite of *upload*.

downloadable font A font that can be transferred (downloaded) to the printer when needed; called a *soft font.*.

downstairs The lower half of the front page of a newspaper; basement.

downtime The time a computer is not operating due to a hardware or software failure.

dpi Acronym for dots per inch, the standard measure of the resolution of imagesetters, laser printers, monitors, and scanners. This represents the total number of dots per square inch. Laser printers generally output at 300 or 600 dpi, while imagesetters output at a resolution that exceed 3000 dpi.

draft Rough, unedited copy.

draft quality Measure of quality for printed output. Usually refers to the result of top-speed printing and therefore not the most precisely defined or fully filled-in characters. Considered acceptable for working copies but not final work.

drag Action of moving the mouse while holding the button down, used to move or manipulate objects on a computer's display screen.

DRAM Short for Dynamic RAM, meaning a type of memory chip that keeps its contents only if supplied with regular clock pulses and a chance to periodically refresh the data internally. DRAM is far less expensive than static RAM (which needs no refreshing) and is the type found in most personal computers.

draw program A program for creating and manipulating object-oriented graphics, as opposed to creating and manipulating pixel images. For example, in a drawing program the user can manipulate an element such as a triangle, or a block of text as an independent object simply by selecting the object and moving it.

drill To bore holes in paper.

driver A program that directs the operation of a device — for example, a computer printer driver.

drop cap An initial letter of a chapter or paragraph enlarged and positioned so that the top of the character is even with the top of the first line and the rest of the character descends into the second and subsequent lines.

Drop caps consist of large capital letters at the beginning of a section of text. The capital letters are aimed at drawing attention to the beginning of the text.

drop cap

drop-down menu A type of menu that drops from the menu bar when requested and remains open without further action until the user closes it or chooses a menu item. Same as *pull-down menu*.

drop folio A folio at the bottom of a page.

dropped letter/initial Initial letter covering more than one line of type.

drop shadow A shadow placed behind an image, slightly off-set horizontally and vertically, that creates the illusion that the topmost image has been lifted off the surface of the page. Drop shadow is very difficult to draw manually, but can be generated by computer graphics instantly. The dropshadow is a feature found in many paint and draw programs.

drop shadow

dtp Abbreviation for Desktop Publishing, the process of setting type and arranging it into page form by means of page composition software and personal computers.

dual kickers A headline style of two small, short heads above the main head — one flush left and one flush right.

dummy A model or mockup of a publication, book, or document showing the placement of pages, headlines, text and pictures.

duotones Halftones printed in two colors, usually black and brown, black and gray, or black and blue.

duplex paper Paper with a different finish or color on each side.

duplex printing Printing a document on both sides of the sheet, so that the verso (left) and recto (right) pages face each other after the document is bound. The main advantage of duplex printing is that it is self-collating, meaning that your documents can arrive ready for a binding.

dust cover A printed cover wrapped loosely around casebound books. Also called *jacket*.

Dvorak keyboard Keyboard arrangement designed by August Dvorak in the 1930s. Provides increased speed and comfort and reduces the rate of errors by placing the most frequently used letters in the center for use by the strongest fingers. See *Maltron keyboard* and *QWERTY keyboard*.

dynamic RAM (DRAM) The most common type of computer memory; the computer must refresh DRAM at frequent intervals. Contrast with static RAM, which is usually faster and does not require refresh circuitry.

ear The projection on letters like the lowercase "g" and "p."

EBCDIC Acronym for Extended Binary Coded Decimal Interchange Code, an 8-bit code used to represent data in large IBM mainframes. EBCDIC can represent up to 256 distinct characters and is the principal code used in many of the current computers.

edge enhancement A way of sharpening up an image, electronically. The program determines where the lines should be and emphasizes the contrast between the object and the background.

edit To modify, refine, or update an emerging design or text on a computer system.

edition One version of a publication, such as the first edition of a book.

editorial A functional page design of magazines where the editor speaks to the readers.

EGA Acronym for Enhanced Graphics Adapter, a video display adapter introduced by IBM in 1984. Video display standard for IBM-compatible microcomputers featuring 640 by 350-pixel resolution. EGA can display no more than 16 colors at once. EGA has been superseded by VGA.

Egyptian A typeface style with slab or square serifs and uniform stroke widths. Also called *square serif*.

A typeface with square serifs and uniform stroke widths.

Egyptian

electronic cottage Concept of permitting workers to remain at home to perform work, using computer terminals connected to a central office.

electronic mail Process of sending, receiving, storing, and forwarding messages in digital form over telecommunication facilities. Also called *E-mail*.

electronic page composition The electronic equivalent of layout.

electronic pasteup See *cut and paste*.

electronic publishing A general term embracing all forms of computerized publication including educational software, CD-ROM, videotape cassettes, videodisks, computer controlled photocopy machines, and computer publishing.

element A block of text, a line, a halftone image, etc.

ellipses Three equally spaced periods (...) used to indicate a pause or an omission of material.

em Horizontal unit of measure referring to the square of the point size. A 10-point em is 10 points high by 10 points wide.

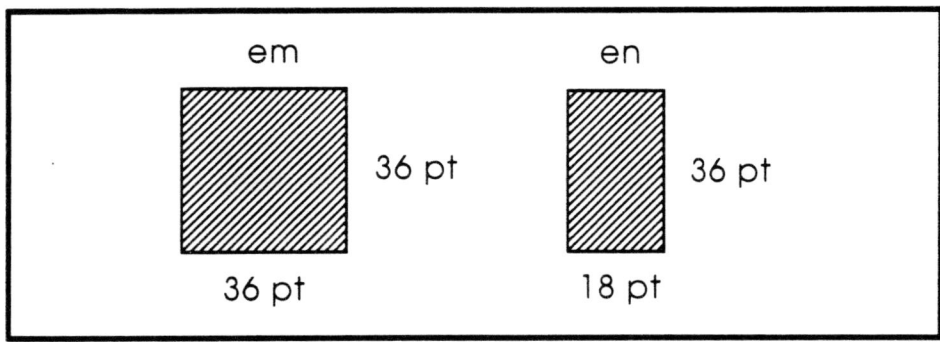

em and *en*

embedded object (1) One or more codes inserted into a document that do not print but direct the application program or printer to control printing and change formats. (2) A document or part of a document that has been embedded in another document.

em dash A long dash — like the ones around this phrase — used to mark a break in a sentence.

em leader Horizontal series of dots or dashes evenly spaced one em from center to center.

em space A fixed amount of white space one em wide.

en A unit of measurement exactly one-half as wide as an em unit.

enamel (1) A coated paper. (2) The coating applied to a paper.

encapsulated PostScript (EPS) A file format developed to facilitate the exchange of PostScript graphics files between applications. Like all PostScript files, EPS files are resolution independent and can be printed by a PostScript printer.

encyclopedia A book or set of books with alphabetically arranged articles on all branches, or on one field, of knowledge. The oldest known encyclopedia was written by Speusippus in Athens, Greece around 370 B.C. The most famous one in the English-speaking world is the *Encyclopedia Britannica*, first published in Edinburgh in 1768.

en dash A dash, longer than a hyphen but shorter than an em dash, sometimes used to join the ends of a range (e.g., 723–8104 or "Chicago–Tokyo flight"), as a minus sign, and in place of a hyphen to join multiword terms (e.g., bit–map).

endleaf Paper at the beginning and end of a hardbound book, half of which is pasted to the cover.

endmatter The pages of a book after the last chapter. Also called *backmatter*.

end notes A style of footnoting where all reference notes are gathered together at the end of the book. See *footnote*.

end user Person who buys and uses computer software or who has contact with computers. A user of a computer.

English finish Smooth finish or uncoated book paper.

enhanced graphics adapter (EGA) A computer graphics board that allows presentation of graphics and text. EGA has been superseded by VGA.

enhanced keyboard A standard keyboard for newer IBM personal computers. It has become the de facto standard for most IBM-compatible keyboards.

enhancement A program that improves the appearance of a typeface or graphic image.

enlarged initial letter The first letter in the first word of a paragraph is set larger than the other letters.

enlarging Increasing the size of a graphic on a page.

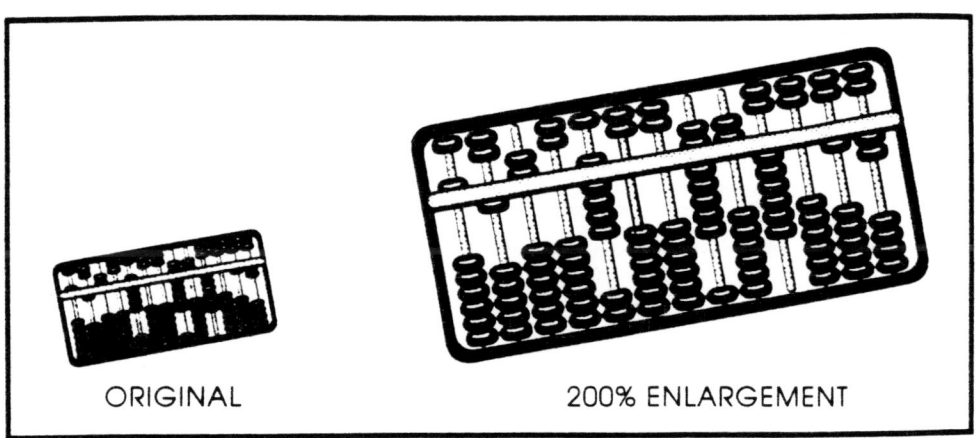
enlarging

en leader Horizontal series of dots or dashes evenly spaced one en from center to center.

en space One half the width of the *em space*; fixed amount of white space one en wide.

ENTER key Special key on some keyboards that means "execute a command." Same as RETURN key on some keyboards.

epilog A concluding section in a book. A summary, or the concluding remarks, of a play or literacy work. A term rarely used in books today. See *prolog*.

EPS Acronym for Encapsulated PostScript. A directly printable PostScript file; the output of a PostScript compatible printer driver captured in a file instead of being sent to a printer.

erase To remove data from storage without replacing it.

eraser Made from a rubber base that erases pen or pencil marks, the eraser is believed to have been invented in the mid-18th century by a physicist named Magalhaens, or Magellan (Portugal, 1722-1790), who perfected numerous instruments for use in physics and astronomy. An eraser was mentioned for the first time in 1770 by the chemist J. Priestley (Great Britain). Today, plastic and synthetic rubber are commonly used to manufacture erasers.

ergonomics Study of the physical relationships between people and their work environment. Adapting machines to the convenience of operators, with

ergonomics

the general aim of maximum efficiency and physical well being. Numeric keypads on standard keyboards, detachable keyboards, and tilting display screens are tangible results. The word comes from ergo (work) and nomics (law or management).

errata A mistake or error in a printed book that is acknowledged on an Errata insert sheet, which is inserted into the book.

error message Printed or displayed statement indicating the computer has detected a mistake or malfunction.

Escape key Standard control key available on most computer keyboards. Used to take control of the computer away from a program, to escape from a specific program, or to stop a program. Abbreviated ESC.

even footer In word processing, a footer that appears on even-numbered pages.

even header In word processing, a header that appears on even-numbered pages.

eWorld An Apple Computer, Inc on-line computer service. Users can get news, information and other services from many concerns.

examination copy A free book given by the book publisher to a teacher or instructor to evaluate for use as a classroom text.

execute To run a program on a computer.

expandability Ability to increase the capability of a computer system by adding modules or devices.

expanded type Wider version of a typeface. Sometimes called "extended type."

ABCDEFGHIJKLMNOPQRSTUVWXYZ
abcdefghijklmnopqrstuvwxyz
expanded type

expansion card A circuit board that plugs into a computer and gives it additional specialized functions (e.g., enhanced graphics, expanded memory, modem).

expansion slot A receptacle inside a computer which is used to plug in printed circuit boards. The number of expansion slots determines the amount of future expansion that is possible within the existing computer system.

exploded pie graph A pie graph in which one or more of the slices has been offset slightly from the others.

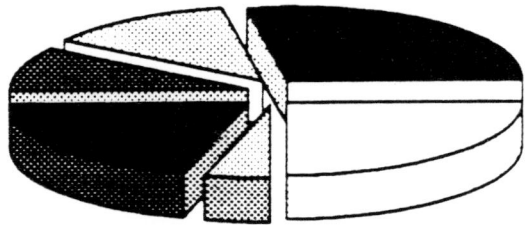

exploded pie graph

exploded view Illustration of a solid construction showing its parts separately, but in positions that indicate their relationships to the whole.

exposure Effect of light on photosensitive materials.

export To transfer information from one system or program to another. Opposite of *import*.

expressed folio A printed page number.

extended A typeface whose letters are stretched (or expanded) horizontally while still retaining their original height.

extended filename A filename that includes the letter of the disk, the directory, the filename, and the file extension all in its name.

extended memory Additional memory chips added to the computer.

extension (1) Additional feature added to a programming language or computer system. Feature beyond what is regularly available in the standard. (2) In reference to a filename that serves to extend or clarify its meaning.

external memory A memory unit equipped with its own case, cables and power supply. Can be extra RAM, ROM, hard disk, floppy disk, or CD-ROM.

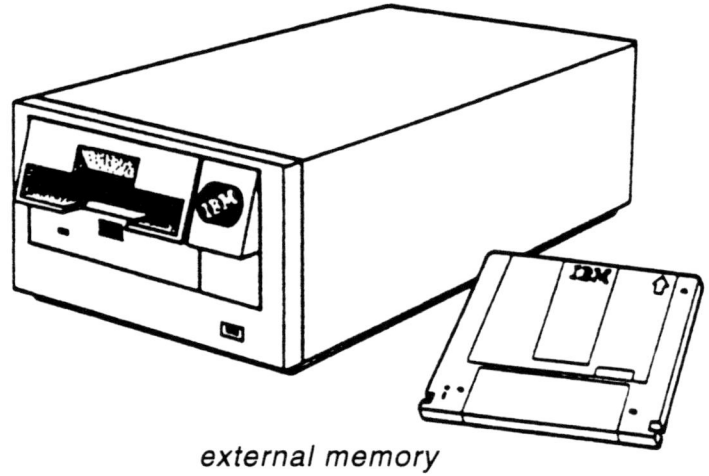

external memory

extra bold A heavier variant of boldface.

F Abbreviation for *face* or *font*.

face (1) A style of type. Short for *typeface*. (2) Edge of a bound publication opposite the spine.

facing pages In a double-sided publication, the two pages that face each other when the publication is open. See *spread*.

facing pages

facsimile (1) The use of computer technology to send digitized text, graphics and charts from one facsimile machine to another. Abbreviated FAX. (2) Approximation of an original, as compared to a duplicate.

fact title In book typography, list of books by same author (faces title page).

fair use The limited use of material from previously copyrighted material, in a manner not considered a violation of copyright, and not requiring permission.

false color Color applied to a black and white image to differentiate features.

false styles Typestyles created by the computer algorithmically rather than using the true style, such as italic, bold, or bold italic.

family A family of variations of characters, usually starting with the medium face and adding bold, italic, light, and other forms. See *typeface family*.

Avant Garde Gothic
Avant Garde Gothic Oblique
Avant Garde Gothic Bold
Avant Garde Gothic Bold Oblique

family

fan The cooling mechanism built into computer cabinets, laser printers and other devices to prevent malfunction due to heat buildup.

f&g A folded and gathered, but not yet bound, copy of a book; a folded and gathered signature of a book.

fanfold paper One long continuous sheet of paper perforated at regular intervals to mark page boundaries and folded fan-style into a stack. Fanfold paper is available with vertical perforations, so the sprocket hole strip can be removed. The paper can be divided on the perforations, thus enabling the paper to be separated into sheets.

fatal error An error in program execution that causes the program to abort; no hope of recovery without rebooting.

fax The use of computer technology to send digitized text, graphics, and charts from one facsimile machine to another. Facsimile.

feathering The process of adding an even amount of space between each line on a page or column to make columns justify vertically on a page.

feature Something special accomplished in a program or hardware device, such as the ability of a paint program to create animation cells, or a word processing program to check the spelling of words.

felt-tipped pen In 1963, Pentel, a Japanese firm, developed the felt pen with an acrylic tip. Pentel also invented the first felt-tipped ballpoint pen in 1973, the Ball Pentel, and in 1981 it launched the first ceramic nib: the Ceramicron.

fiberboard Paperboard made of laminated sheets of heavily pressed fiber.

field Single piece of information, the smallest unit normally manipulated by a database management system. In a personnel file, the person's name and age would be separate fields. A record is made up of one or more fields.

figure General term for any illustration, photograph, table, or any other visual element in a technical publication.

figure space An en space; the space occupied by a number; used to line up columns of figures.

file A collection of related information in the system which may be accessed by a unique name. May be stored on a disk, tape, or other storage media.

file compression See *compression*.

file deletion Removing the file name from the directory.

file fragmentation A condition in which there are many scattered areas of storage that are too small to be used productively.

file locking Protects shared files by allowing only one user at a time to make changes.

file maintenance Updating of a file to reflect the effects of nonperiodic changes by adding, altering, or deleting data.

file management Creation and maintenance of files by means of computer.

filename Alphanumeric characters used to identify a particular file.

file protection Technique or device used to prevent accidental erasure of data from a file.

file recovery A broad term used to describe any method for getting back a file that has been lost or damaged.

file server The central repository of shared files and applications in a computer network.

filigree initials

filigree initials Initial letters surrounded by fine ornate lines.

fill (1) To place a pattern, gray scale, graduated range, or color in a defined region.

film laminate See *laminate*.

film recorder An output device that takes a 35 mm slide picture from an image file which has been created using a page layout program. Widely used in producing a presentation-quality hardcopy. Film recorders offer both high resolution (up to 2000 dots per inch) and a true color reproduction capability (up to 6 million simultaneous colors). Lines show perfectly smooth edges, and colors blend imperceptibly in film recorder images.

filter A software function that modifies an image by altering the gray values of certain pixels.

finder A system program that provides the "desktop" metaphor you encounter when a Macintosh microcomputer is booted up. The finder presents icons (little pictures) depicting applications, documents, file folders, and a garbage can that can be used to discard unwanted files. This highly visual interface program keeps the user from having to type commands directly to the operating system.

first proofs Proofs submitted for checking by copy editors, proofreaders, and so forth.

fixed disk Same as *hard disk*.

fixed space A constant-width blank space. The most common widths are the "em" and "en." See *em space* and *en space*.

flag The nameplate of a newspaper or newsletter used on page one.

flat Term describing low value contrasts.

flatbed plotter Digital plotter using plotting heads that move over a flat surface in both vertical and horizontal directions. The size of the bed determines the maximum size sheet of paper that can be drawn.

flatbed scanner A scanner with a glass surface upon which you place material to be scanned. Because the original never moves during the scanning process, flatbeds produce more precise results than sheetfed scanners. The scanner can transform a full-page (8.5x11-inch) graphic or page of text into a digitized file.

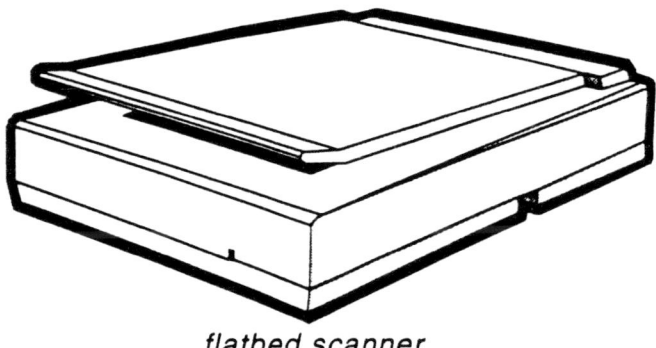
flatbed scanner

flatness The amount of calculation that a PostScript interpreter has to do to create a curve. Higher flatness values mean less calculation, faster printing, but rougher curves.

flex A means of automatically suppressing small details such as cupped serifs that would print poorly at small sizes. At large sizes or high resolutions, the details are automatically reinstated.

flicker Undesirable, unsteady lighting of a display due to inadequate refresh rate and/or fast persistence. Occurs whenever the refresh speed is not fast enough to compensate for natural luminance delay on the screen.

flier See *flyer*.

flipping Manipulating an image so that it is reversed either horizontally or vertically.

flop To reverse an image so that it appears as a mirror image.

floppy disk

floppy disk Floppy disks are a form of computer storage medium consisting of a thin flexible disk covered with magnetic oxide held inside a protective sleeve within which it can be rotated. They are lightweight, cheap and portable. Floppy disks, universally used on microcomputers, were invented in 1950 at the Imperial University in Tokyo by Yoshiro Nakamats, an inventor who boasts of having 2,360 patents for objects as diverse as golf clubs and loudspeakers. He granted the sales license for the disk to the IBM Corporation.

floptical disk Developed by Insite Peripherals, the floptical disk drive can store 20.8 megabytes on standard 3.5-inch diskettes. Moreover, it is fully compatible with earlier formats: 720 kilobytes and 1.44 megabytes. This achievement is due to the use of optical recording techniques.

floret A flower-like typographic ornament.

floret

flow (1) In a page layout program, importing text into a specified area. (2) In a graphics program or page layout program, wrapping text around a graphic object on the same page. (3) To pour text into a column.

flush left Pertaining to text that is aligned to the left margin but need not be aligned to the right margin.

flush right Pertaining to text that is aligned to the right margin but need not be aligned to the left margin.

dhncvjk sjsdjdjdj dkeewo shemvot mkg siere woc diemxiw dierrjpa eucn cmddiekwpdk sjd wuxmd fjdjfkgglfieofkriglfrspem eucmslozxpqa mnsue shri wixmd kfieps adqwpcmtu eidlviwmclaw nmb sskdk ryxnwaskjflvmnbwy	dhncvjk sjsdjdjdj dkeewo shemvot mkg siere woc diemxiw dierrjpa eucn cmddiekwpdk sjd wuxmd fjdjfkgglfieofkriglfrspem eucmslozxpqa mnsue shri wixmd kfieps adqwpcmtu eidlviwmclaw nmb sskdk ryxnwaskjflvmnbwy
flush left	*flush right*

flyer Small poster or advertising handout; a single-sided publication. Also called a leaflet.

fly leaf The first sheet in hardbound books that is attached to the inside covers.

folder A subdirectory on the Macintosh computer.

folio A page number. Right-hand pages are odd; left-hand pages are even.

folio count Number of pages in a publication.

font A complete assortment or set of all the characters (letters, numbers, punctuation and symbols) of a particular typeface, all of one size and style (e.g., 12 pt. Bookman, 18 pt. Helvetica, 36 pt. Cooper Black, 8 pt. Times Roman). Two types of fonts exist: bit-mapped fonts and outline fonts.

ABCDEFGHIJKLMNOPQRSTUVWXYZ
abcdefghijklmnopqrstuvwxyz
1234567890&?!$(.,;:)

font

font cache A temporary storage place for characters that have been converted from an outline format to a bitmap format for imaging on the screen or printer at a particular size, orientation, and resolution.

font cartridge A set of fonts for one or more typefaces contained in a module that plugs into a laser printer slot. The fonts are stored in a ROM chip within the cartridge.

font downloader An application that allows you to manually download outline printer fonts and perform other printer management functions.

font family A set of fonts in several sizes and weights that share the same typeface.

Times Roman

Times Italic

Times Bold

Times Bold Italic

font family

> Serif
>
> Sans Serif
>
> DISPLAY

font groups

font groups Fonts are often divided into three groups. Serif, Sans Serif, and Display. Type styles in the Serif group have additional strokes (serifs) at the top and bottom of each letter. Type styles in the Sans Serif group do not have serifs. Display (or decorative) type styles can be either Serif or Sans Serif. Type styles in this group are used when you want to create a dramatic effect in headings, logos, and product names. They are rarely used in long passages of text since they are typically difficult to read.

font smoothing In laser printers, the reduction of aliasing and other distortions when graphics or text are printed.

font substitution Using an alternate font when the one you specified isn't available.

fontware An electronic type font.

foot The margin at the bottom of a page.

footer Text printed at the bottom of every page of a document, such as page numbers. Also called a *footline*.

footline A repeating footer at the bottom of pages of text, often listing a publication name, chapter name, or other information. Also called a *footer*.

footnote A note positioned at the bottom of the page. It is a comment, explanation, or citation that explains text. See *end notes*.

footprint The surface area occupied by a computer or peripheral. A small computer is said to have a small footprint. A machine with a large footprint may need a desk to itself.

foreground processing Automatic execution of computer programs that have been designed to preempt the use of computing facilities.

foreign rights The subsidiary rights that allows a book to be translated into other languages or published in other countries.

foreword A short introduction to a book, written by a person other than the author. A foreword often explains or praises a book.

formal balance Formal balance centers all elements on the vertical center of the page. Formal designs are common for business communications. Announcements of formal events such as weddings and ceremonies often employ formal balance. See *informal balance*.

format (1) Specific arrangement of data. (2) Programming associated with setting up text arrangements for output. (3) Preparing a floppy disk for use so that the operating system can write information on it. Formatting erases any previous information there. (4) A pattern for the display, storage, or printing of data. (5) Size, style, shape, layout, or typography.

forms program A desktop publishing program with one specific task — to create and modify business forms.

fountain pen Nobody knows exactly how far back the idea of adding an ink reservoir to a quill pen goes. In her *Memoirs*, Catherine the Great of Russia noted that she used an "endless quill" in 1748. Was she referring to one of the first pens? Between 1880 and 1900, fountain pen inventions proliferated; more than 400 patents were registered. The inventor of the first true fountain pen was Lewis E. Waterman (U.S.), an insurance broker, who had had enough of almost losing contracts due to malfunctioning pens. In 1884, he obtained the first patent for what was to become the Waterman Regular. The ink cartridge was invented by M. Perrand in 1927, and patented in 1935.

4-across-5 A design in which four columns of type are spread across a five-column area. Also referred to as 4-on-5.

four color process printing A printing process where images such as paintings and color photographs are reproduced by means of four separate printing plates. Each plate prints one of the four standard printing inks, called process colors — process blue (cyan), process red (magenta), process yellow, and process black.

fraction bar The oblique line used to separate one element from another in type.

fragmentation The condition of having different parts of the same file scattered throughout a disk.

frame A rectangular box used to hold text and pictures; specially designed area marked on a screen for unique treatment. An entire page may be considered as a frame or selected areas can be framed.

frame grabber A computer utility that freezes one image from a video program, digitizes it, and inserts it into a page layout.

Frankfurt Book Fair International book fair. Frankfurt was a major center of international trade in the late Middle Ages, and books were sold at the fairs there before the end of the fifteenth century. Frankfurt always had a truly international flavor, for although many German books were sold, its primary importance was as a market place for Latin books with their Europe-wide audience. The Frankfurt Fair also became the major center for dealing in printing type and equipment. Today, the Frankfurt Fair is an annual gathering at which publishers from all over the world display their wares and deal in rights sales. See *book fairs*.

freeware Software provided by a vendor at no charge. Freeware developers often retain all rights to their software thus preventing users from copying it or distributing it further.

French fold A double fold in which the sheet is folded once vertically and once horizontally.

French spacing The practice of inserting additional space behind punctuation symbols, and before starting the next sentence.

fresh air White space.

friendly In computer jargon, equipment and software that are easy to understand and use.

frontispiece A picture, photograph, sketch or other drawing facing the title page in a book.

frontlist New books published by a book publisher. Contrast with *backlist*.

frontmatter The elements of a book which precede the first page of the first chapter, i.e., half title page, frontispiece, title page, copyright page, dedication, table of contents, table of illustrations, acknowledgment, introduction, foreword and preface.

full bleed A graphic or photograph that bleeds to the edge of the trimmed page.

full-justified Copy aligned on both the left and right margins.

full measure A line set so that it fills the entire space between left and right margins.

full page display A monitor that allows viewing an entire page (8.5 in. x 11 in. vertical page) at actual size. Makes for greater flexibility and ease in desktop publishing or word processing applications.

full page display

function keys Specially designed keys that, when pressed, initiates some function on a computer keyboard, word processor, or graphics terminal. Most software assign function keys (F1, F2, etc.) for common tasks, but not universally. For example, in one word processor, F4 might mean "save file," while in a different word processor, F4 might mean "increase size of character." These special keys are programmed to execute commonly used commands.

Fust, John Between 1440 and 1460, one of three people living in Mentz, Germany to whom the invention of printing is credited. The other two being Johann Gutenberg and Peter Schoeffer. See *Gutenberg, Johann* and *Schoeffer, Peter*.

G

gagline Caption for a cartoon.

galley Refers to typeset material which is not yet pasted up into page form; typeset material in column form. The proof of a page provided for final editing before final printing.

gathering Putting signatures in proper order for binding.

GBC See *comb binding*.

genre Category of publications such as reference, science fiction, romance, how-to, mystery, travelogue, or technical.

geometric Serif or sans serif designs composed of visually geometric character shapes. For example, Avant Garde or Futura.

Avant Garde
geometric

ghost A faint second image that appears close to the primary image on a display or printout.

ghost icon An outline of an icon or window used to show the current position of the icon or window as it is being dragged to a new location on the desktop.

GIF A graphics format often used for pictures that are transmitted by modem. Especially popular with computer bulletin boards and information services such as CompuServe. Acronym for Graphic Interchange Format.

gigabyte Specifically, 1,073,741,824 bytes. More loosely, one billion bytes, one million kilobytes, or one thousand megabytes. Abbreviated GB.

gimcrack A typographic ornament.

glitch Popular term for a temporary or random error, problem or malfunction in hardware, such as a malfunction caused by a power surge.

gloss A characteristic of paper or paper coatings (laminating film, UV coating, or varnish) that reflects a relatively large amount of light.

glossary An alphabetical list of words giving definitions relevant to a specific topic. It is often a section of backmatter where terms used in the book are defined.

"good enough" color A phrase used for color printing that does not require an exact color match. Relatively easy to produce with current desktop color resources.

gothic In modern usage, Gothic refers to sans serif monoweight letters. Futura and News Gothic are examples.

gppm Acronym for graphics pages per minute, the speed at which a laser printer can print pages of graphics images.

grabber (1) A device for capturing data, i.e., a video digitizer. (2) A computer program that takes a "snapshot" of the currently displayed screen image by transferring a portion of video memory to a file on disk.

grabber hand In graphics programs, an on-screen image of a hand that you can position with the mouse to move selected units of graphics or text from place to place on-screen.

gradation Range of values from white to black.

gradient A gradual change in color intensity, or from one color to another.

grain Predominant direction in which the fibers line up when a sheet of paper is made. In some papers the grain runs along the length of the sheet (grain long) while in others it runs across the width (grain short). A book should be bound so that its spine aligns with the grain. Otherwise the pages will not lie flat but will curl inward from top to bottom.

grammar checker A program that checks for subject-verb disagreement, awkward phrases, wordiness, incomplete sentences and other grammar problems.

graph A pictorial representation of information.

graphical user interface (GUI) A type of display format that enables the user to choose commands, start programs, and see lists of files and other options by pointing to pictorial representations (icons) and lists of menu items on the screen. Graphical user interfaces are used on the Apple Macintosh microcomputer, by the Microsoft Windows and Presentation Manager for IBM-compatible microcomputers, and other systems.

graphic display resolution The number of pixels displayed horizontally by vertically on a graphic screen display.

graphic display system An integrated system comprised of a monitor, graphics display card, and software.

graphic display system

graphic element A generic term for art in a layout.

graphic font A font consisting of pictures rather than alphabetic characters; an ornamental or novelty font.

graphic image Any graphically defined shape, such as a font character, a piece of clip art, and so on.

graphics Any computer-generated picture produced on a screen, paper, or film. Graphics range from simple line or bar graphs to colorful and detailed images. All computers have some amount of graphics capability, but now most feature high-resolution graphics in color, and printed pictures can also be produced in color.

graphics

graphics accelerator An expansion board that includes a graphics coprocessor. The coprocessor is a microprocessor specially designed for fast graphics processing. Graphics acceleration calculate pixel values, and write them into the frame buffer, freeing up the central processing unit for other operations.

graphics adapters CGA-EGA-VGA adapters that must be matched with compatible monitors. Note the alphabetical order — it happens to match their order of age and sophistication. CGA was first. EGA was the new standard for a long while. VGA is now the popular standard for color presentations. VGA has higher resolution modes, and sharper text and image quality.

graphics coprocessor A special microprocessor chip, mounted on some video adaptors, that can generate graphical images, thereby freeing the computer for other work.

graphics program A computer program that aids computer users in producing computer generated images. Pictures can be entered into the computer using input devices such as mice, graphics tablets or light pens, and existing pictures on paper can be scanned into the computer using digitized scanners. Once stored in the computers memory pictures can be manipulated in a variety of ways and printed on paper, display screen or film.

graphics tablet

graphics tablet Input device that converts graphic and pictorial data into binary inputs for use in a computer. Provides an efficient method of converting object shapes into computer-storable information. Utilizes a flat tablet and a stylus for graphic input.

grayscale Showing an image using a specified number of gray values, black and white values between 0 and 100%.

grayscale monitor A monitor capable of displaying a full range of shades from white to black on the display screen.

gray value An indication of the level of gray in a particular pixel. A pixel that is 20 percent gray is lighter than a pixel that is 50 percent gray.

greeking Nonsense type or marks in the correct size and style used to simulate the appearance of actual text. Greeking shows the overall appearance of a printed page without showing the actual text. Greeking is the representation of text by type that has no meaning.

grid A configuration of horizontal and vertical lines that defines the page layout and facilitates accurate and consistent placement of elements on the page. A grid design is a basic design structure where elements are fit into imaginary rectangular areas on the page.

group To combine two or more objects so that they act as one object.

GUI See *graphical user interface*.

guide (1) A series of nonprinting dotted or dashed lines that can be created to help with alignment. Most page composition programs feature horizontal and vertical column guides, margin guides, and ruler guides. (2) A publication that gives a reader instructions about using a product. (3) Template for design.

Johann Gutenberg

Gutenberg, Johann (1398-1468) A craftsman and inventor, born in the year 1398 in the city of Mentz, Germany, originated a method of printing from movable type that was used without important change until the 20th century. In 1438 he entered a contract with three others to develop a refined printing technique. He is thought to have completed the printing of the Bible in 1455, the first book printed from type. To do so, he had to develop methods of typesetting, imposition and printing. Although it is the latter which has attracted attention, the pre-printing stages were in some ways more difficult, for they involved wholly new techniques and equipment. After finishing the Bible, Gutenberg never again had any contact with the craft which he had invented and which was to revolutionize the world into which he had been born. See *Fust, John* and *Schoeffer, Peter*.

gutter (1) The margin at the binding edge of a page. (2) White space between a multiple-column page layout.

hairline (1) A thin stroke usually common to serif typestyles. (2) A fine rule, generally 0.25 point. Called a hairline rule.

h & j Abbreviation for hyphenation and justification. The arrangement of text evenly in a column (justification), usually requiring the breaking of words at their appropriate syllable breaks (hyphenation).

half title page In book typography, a book title alone on a page; a single page of front matter. The half title page precedes the full title page.

halftone Simulating a continuous tone image using various sized dots. Larger dots represent darker areas, smaller dots represent lighter areas. Computers and laser printers gather groups of same-sized dots or bits to simulate these various sized dots. See *dithering*.

halftone

hammer A short one-line head, which is twice as large as the main head, that is placed below and indented to the right.

hand-held scanner An optical scanner that is operated by manually running a scanning head over an image. Small rollers on the bottom of the scanning head serve to guide the hand movement.

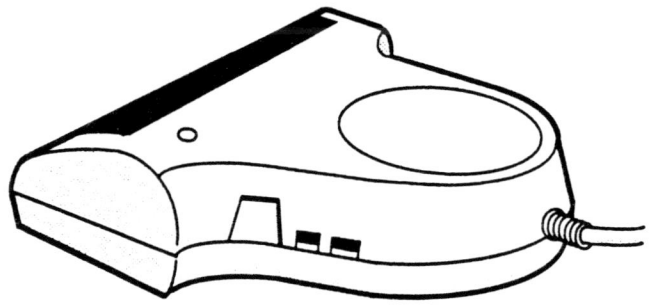

hand-held scanner

handle (1) In computer graphics, a small square associated with a graphical object that can be used to move or reshape the image. (2) A number that can be used to uniquely identify an object.

hanging indent A paragraphing style with a full-measure first line and indented succeeding lines (called turnover lines). Also called hanging paragraph.

> Helen Keller was born in Tuscumbia, Alabama in 1880. She was deprived of sight, hearing and the ability to speak before the age of two due to a severe illness. Her life represents one of the most extraordinary examples of a person who was able to transcend her physical handicaps.
> Through the constant and patient instruction of Anne Sullivan, Helen Keller not only learned to read, write and speak, but went on to graduate *cum laude* from Radcliffe College in 1904.

hanging indent

hanging punctuation A typesetting practice that allows certain punctuation marks to extend into the margin, beyond the second and succeeding lines.

hardcopy Computer output onto a tangible substrate, such as paper or film.

hard disk Fast auxiliary storage device either mounted in its own case or permanently mounted inside a computer. A single hard disk has storage capacity of several million characters or bytes of information. This storage media makes computers usable in the real world. Contrast with *floppy disk*.

hard hyphen A "typed-in" hyphen which is always printed. Contrast with soft hyphens and discretionary hyphens, which print only if the justification of the column forces a word to break.

hard space In word processing programs, a space specially formatted so that the program does not introduce a line break at the space's location. Hard spaces often are used to keep two-words together, such as System 7 or sans serif.

hardware The physical components of a computer system. Contrast with *software*.

head Headline; also the top of a page.

headband A decorative band at the top and bottom of the spine of a hardcover book.

head crash Collision of the read/write head with the recording surface of a hard disk, resulting in loss of data. Usually caused by contamination of the disk, such as from a tiny particle of smoke or dust or from a fingerprint.

header Top margin of a page, usually the title of the book, the name of the chapter, the page number, and so on. See *running head*.

heading In a book or magazine, the display type copy which introduces chapters or sections.

headletter The typeface used for headlines.

headline Display type, usually at the top of a project, used to attract attention. It is the most prominent element of type in a piece of printing.

head margin The space between the top of the page and the first line of text.

head trim The side of gathered signatures that is trimmed before being bound.

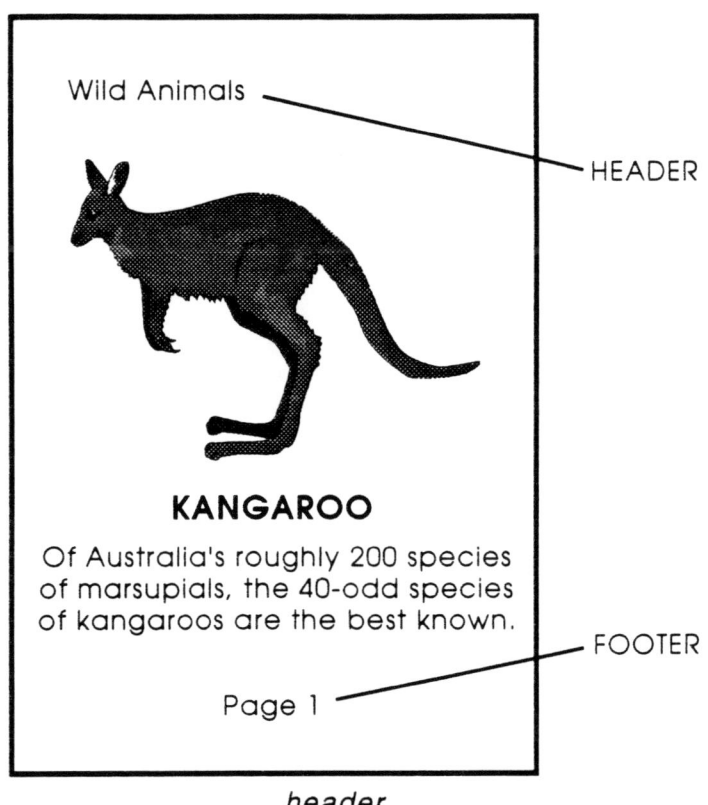

header

heavy A particular weight of a typeface, thicker than bold.

help (1) Handy function available on many systems. Supplies the user with additional information on how the system or program works. (2) On screen reference material providing assistance with the program.

help balloon An operating system and application program user help aid that tags a desired object on screen with a comic book style "balloon" full of information on how to use that object.

helvetica A widely used sans serif typeface. It was designed in 1957 by Max Meidinger. Helvetica has enjoyed phenomenal success in all typesetting technologies. Its use has been extended considerably in desktop publishing by its large library of variants.

hickey A printing imperfection; a white ring with a dark center, usually caused by dust.

hidden character A character that is not normally printed or displayed; for example, in a word processor, an embedded control character.

hidden file Hidden files occupy disk space but do not appear in directory listings. Files are hidden to prevent their display or change. Sometimes called invisible files. You cannot display, erase, or copy hidden files.

hidden line (1) When displaying a three-dimensional object, any line that would normally be obscured from the viewer's sight by the mass of the object itself, visible as a result of the projection. (2) Lines that have been drawn on the screen in background color and will not become visible until the colors are switched. (3) Lines of a diagram that are invisible.

high-bulk paper Paper made relatively thick in proportion to its basic weight, thus yielding fewer pages per inch. High-bulk paper is used to make a book thicker than it would be if printed on lower-bulk paper.

high-density disk A floppy disk that holds more information than a double-density disk.

highlighting (1) Process of making a display segment stand out by underlining or reversing the background and the character images, such as light characters on a dark background, or creating a color combination that draws attention to it. (2) Highlighting is often used in word processing and page design programs as a means of selecting characters that are to be deleted, copied, or otherwise acted upon.

highlight The brightest part of a photograph or halftone.

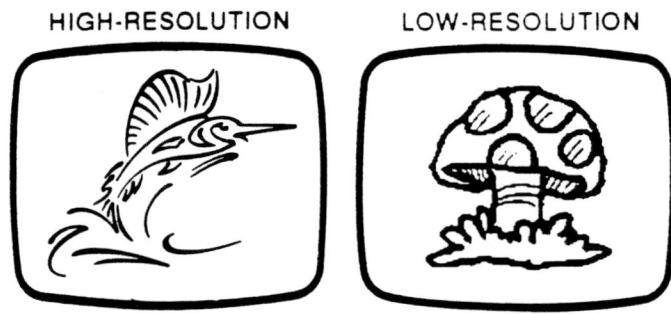

high-resolution

high-resolution (1) Pertaining to the quality and accuracy of detail that can be represented by a graphics display. Resolution quality depends upon the number of basic image-forming units (pixels) within a picture image — the greater the number, the higher the resolution. High-resolution pictures, produced by a large number of pixels, are sharper than low-resolution pictures. (2) In printing, resolution is defined as the number of dots per inch (dpi) that are printed. In general, laser printing is usually 300 or 600 dpi, imagesetters can produce output at 1000 dpi, 2000 dpi, or more.

hinting The process by which a font is slightly altered at print time. The alterations improve the regularity of the final character shape and produce better looking characters.

hints Special PostScript Type 1 and TrueType font information that conveys important typographic information about a particular font or a particular attribute of a specific character in a font. The hints are used by the PostScript interpreter during the rasterizing process to improve the appearance of characters at low resolutions and small point sizes.

home computer A personal computer designed and priced for use in the home.

home key Keyboard function that directs the cursor to its home position, usually in the top left portion of the display screen.

homographs Words that are spelled the same but pronounced and hyphenated differently.

hood A three-sided box around a headline.

horizontal grid A series of horizontal guidelines that help with alignment.

horizontal makeup A layout design that places most body type in flat, shallow areas.

horizontal ruler An electronic ruler that is usually displayed across the top of the display screen.

horizontal scaling Mathematically stretching letterforms horizontally, making them narrower or wider.

horizontal spacing The process of adjusting the spacing between all characters of a font set. See *tracking*.

hot spot The single pixel that is activated by clicking the mouse on it.

housekeeping Computer operations that do not directly contribute toward the desired results, but are a necessary part of a program, such as initialization, set-up, and clean-up operations.

house paper Paper kept in stock by a printer and suitable for a variety of printing jobs. Customers usually pay less for the house paper than for comparable paper because printers buy house paper in large quantities.

hue A specific color such as blue or green. Burgundy, crimson, cardinal, rose, and rhodamine are all red hues.

hung punctuation Punctuation at the beginning or end of a line set outside the line measure.

hung system A computer that has experienced a system failure sufficiently grave to prevent further processing.

HyperCard An implementation of a hypertext system for the Apple Macintosh family of computers. A HyperCard document consists of a series of cards collected together in a stack; each card can contain text, graphics and sound. Items on the cards can be linked together in a variety of different ways.

hypermedia A term describing hypertext-based systems that combine text, graphics, sound, and video with traditional data. In a hypertext system, you select a word or phrase and give a command to see related text. In a hypermedia system, such a command reveals related graphics images, sounds, and even snippets of animation or video. HyperCard is an example of a hypermedia application.

hypertext An assembly of images, sound and text connected by electronic links, which facilitates nonlinear reading and writing.

hyphen Short dash that connects some words into compounds or divides a word at the end of a line.

hyphenate To insert a hyphen into a word so that the word can be broken between two lines of text.

hyphenation In page layout and word processing programs, an automatic operation that hyphenates words on certain lines to improve word spacing. Hyphenation is the process of breaking words which do not fit in the space available at the end of a line.

I

I-beam pointer In a graphical user interface, a special pointer shaped like a capital "I" that indicates the insertion point for text editing.

IBM PC compatible A term for personal computers that adhere closely to the functionality of personal computers in the IBM PC family. PC compatibles, as opposed to "clones," have never necessarily had to look like standard IBM PC designs, and some manufacturers have insisted on incorporating proprietary, non-standard features in their "compatibles" even while maintaining general compatibility with the MS-DOS, Intel-based features of the IBM PC family.

IBM Personal Computer August 12, 1981, came and went, but nothing would ever be the same again. That day, the IBM Corporation introduced a Personal Computer based on the Intel 8088 microprocessor. The machine went on to become the most significant technology to hit the world since the telephone. Although the IBM PC was not the first, it legitimized the machines in the computer market. It has transformed the way millions of people work, spawned new industries and made computer technology less mysterious. The PC created the home computer movement, allowing people to work out of their living room and "commute" by sending reports to the office over the phone. IBM set the stage for clones when it announced the PC by deciding not to block other companies from providing software or accessories for its PC. It reasoned that if the technology was "open," or non-proprietary, the market for the machines would grow faster. But that decision soon led to the creation of clones of the entire computer. Today, every nation from Hong Kong to Hungary has a local industry cranking out inexpensive PC clones. There are three machines in the PC line: IBM PC, IBM PC-XT and IBM PC-AT.

IBM Personal System/2 (PS/2) A series of personal computers from IBM Corporation introduced in 1987. These computers were designed to replace the IBM Personal Computer line: IBM PC, IBM PC-XT, IBM PC-AT. The PS/2 machines are based on the Intel 8086, 80286, 80386, and 80486 microprocessors. The IBM PS/2 runs all or almost all the software developed for the IBM Personal Computer.

icon A tiny on-screen pictorial representation of a software function. A symbol used on the display screen to represent some feature of the program. For example, in one program, an icon representing a waste-paper basket is selected if you want to erase information. Many workstations in a networking environment, for instance, use a mailbox icon to symbolize an electronic mail-reading utility. Non-technical people find symbols easier to understand than technical words. Icons can be used to visually represent ideas, concepts, messages, functions, or objects.

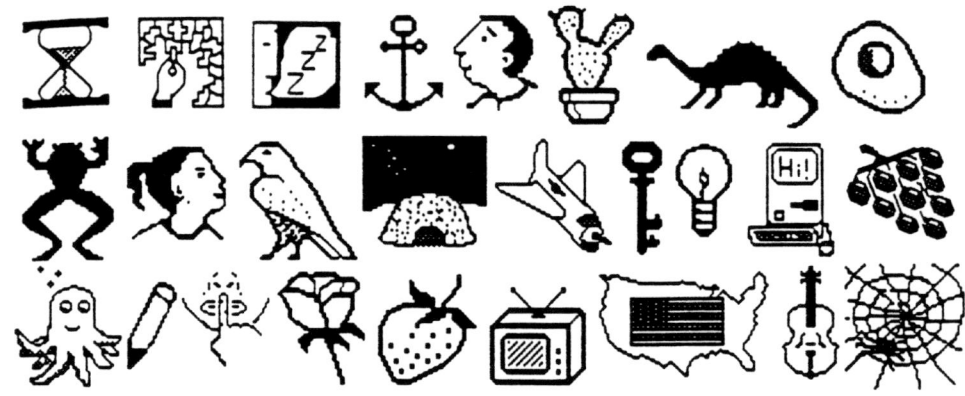

icon

ideograph A symbol that represents an idea.

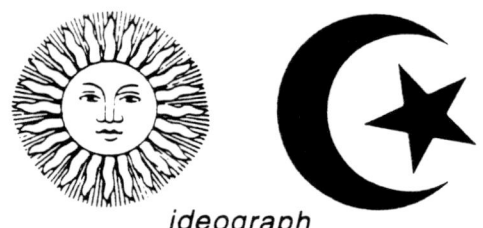

ideograph

idle time Time that a computer system is available for use, but is not in actual operation.

illegal character Character or combination of bits not accepted by the computer as a valid or known representation.

illustration Artwork used to describe, explain or attract attention.

illustration program A program for creating and manipulating object-oriented graphics, as opposed to creating and manipulating pixel images. See *draw program* and *paint program*.

image (1) A picture created with a painting or drawing program or a scanner. (2) The computerized representation of a picture or graphic.

image area That area of a page on which a mark can be made. The image area of a laser printer is about 8 inches by 10.5 inches.

image compression As applied to graphics computer systems and scanners, encoding the data describing an image in a more compact form to reduce storage requirements or transmission time.

image cropping See *cropping*.

image enhancement The process of improving the appearance of all or part of a graphics image through such techniques as coloring, shading, highlighting, edge enhancement, gray-scale manipulation, zooming, reverse video, blinking, smoothing, or sharpening.

image processing Method for processing pictorial information by a computer system. Involves inputting graphics information into a computer system, storing it, working with it, and outputting it to an output device.

image resolution The actual resolution in dots per inch of an image that has been scanned or transmitted by video into a computer environment.

imagesetter A typesetting device that can transfer output of a desktop publishing system directly to paper or film. Imagesetters commonly print at high resolution (from 1200 dpi to over 3000 dpi). Imagesetters are professional typesetting machines that use chemical photo-reproduction techniques to produce high resolution output.

impact printer Data printout device that imprints by momentary pressure of raised type against paper, using ink or ribbon as a color medium. Contrast with *nonimpact printer*.

import To bring information from one system or program into another. PageMaker, for example, can import EPS files created by Adobe Illustrator, MacPaint files created by SuperPaint or text files created by Microsoft Word.

imported text Text created in a word processing program that is electronically transferred into a desktop publishing program.

impose To arrange pages in the proper order and orientation for printing.

impression In printing, one impression equals one sheet of paper passing through a printing unit.

imprint A book trade term. The imprint is the publisher's name, and usually its location, printed at the foot of the title page.

inch size The measurement, in inches, of the vertical size of a font. Same as point size except the dimension is given in inches instead of points.

increment The distance between tick marks on a ruler using any given standard of measurement such as inches, picas or millimeters.

indent A space, usually to the right of the left margin, specifying the first character of a line. Indents placed to the left of a left margin are termed hanging indents. Indents are usually used to mark the beginning of a new paragraph, or to offset a block of text, such as a quotation.

> Celebrated as both a technological genius and a folk hero, Henry Ford was the creative force in the automotive industry. His innovations changed the economic and social character of his country - and the world.
> Ford developed the mass-produced "Model T" automobile and sold it at a price the average person could afford. Use of the assembly line in mass production saved time and money and allowed Ford to offer more cars to the American public at a lower price than anyone before him. More than 15 million "Model T's" were sold in the United States between 1908 and 1927.

indent

indention A form of placement for text and display showing the relation of items, one to another. The simplest indent is the "paragraph," which denotes the beginning of a text block. The indent should be proportional to the line length: 1 em space (under 24 picas), 1.5 em spaces (25-36 picas), 2 em spaces (37 picas or more).

index A section of backmatter listing the page locations of specific subjects in a book. The index will probably be referred to more often than any other item in the backmatter, which is why it must be placed in the most convenient position — at the very back, after all the items.

infection The presence within a computer system of a virus.

infographics Charts and graphs that graphically portray information.

informal balance Informal balance allows elements to be off center, but other principles are employed to create a feeling of balance or equilibrium on the page. See *formal balance*.

information Meaningful and useful facts that are extracted from data fed to a computer. Processed data; data that is organized, meaningful, and useful.

infringement Violation of another person's copyright ownership, by using copyrighted material without permission to an extent that does not constitute fair use.

initial cap The use of a very large, graphic character to begin the text at the start of a book chapter, section or occasional paragraph. Initial caps are measured in depth. A 4-line initial cap is 4 lines of text in depth. Also called *drop caps*.

One of the greatest scientific minds of all time, Albert Einstein is best known for his contributions to the field of physics. Born in Germany in 1879, Einstein received his diploma from the Swiss Federal Polytechnic School in Zurich, where he trained as a teacher in physics and mathematics.

initial caps

initialization Process of formatting a diskette so that it is ready for use. Initialization erases any previous information that happens to be on the diskette.

ink The Chinese invented ink in 2500 B.C. It was made with smoke, glue and aromatic substances. Evidence has been found in Egyptian hypogea of papyrus covered in black or red ink applied with a reed and even a quill pen.

ink jet printer A printer that sprays ink from jet nozzles onto the paper. A nozzle emits a continuous stream of ink droplets that are selectively guided

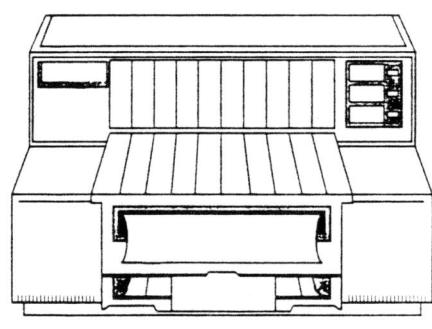

ink jet printer

either to the paper or to a gutter where they may be recycled for re-use or sent into a discard container. Ink jet printers produce high-quality printouts.

inline A typeface design with a white line cut through the stems of characters. The type style resembles a chisel effect as if chipped out of stone. Inline typefaces are classic in their appearance and should be used in small doses for major display purposes. Examples are Antique Roman, Bodoni Open and Caslon Inline.

ABCDEFGHIJK
inline

in print A book that is currently available from a publisher.

input Introduction of data from an external storage medium into a computer's internal storage unit. Contrast with *output*.

input device A hardware device that enables the user to communicate with a computer system. Examples of input devices are keyboard, mouse, light pen, track ball, or graphics tablet. Contrast with *output device*.

input/output device Unit used to get data from the human user into the central processing unit, and to transfer data from the computer's internal storage to some storage or output device. See *input device, output device,* and *peripheral equipment*.

input/output device

insert (1) To create and place entities, figures, text, or information on a CRT or into an emerging design on the display. (2) The addition of text to a document. (3) A group of pages placed in a book, i.e., a color page insert, an art gallery insert, etc.

insertion point Position at which text is entered into a document. It is usually a blinking vertical bar indication where the next keyboarded or pasted text will appear.

inset initial A large letter placed into body type.

inside margin The margin along the binding edge of the page, which is the left margin of a right-hand page or the right margin of a left-hand page.

installation General term for a particular computer system.

installation program A program that prepares a software program to run in the computer. It customizes elements of the new program so a specific computer system can use it.

instructor's manual A guide that supplements a specific textbook. The guide is used by college instructor's to aid them in using the textbook in the classroom.

intaglio printing A printing technique where the design to be printed is recessed into a surface and the hollows are filled with ink.

integrated circuit (IC) An electronic circuit etched on a tiny germanium or silicon chip. Integrated circuits are categorized by the number of elements (transistors, resistors, etc.) they hold.

integrated software An applications software package containing programs to perform more than one function. The package typically includes related word processing, spreadsheet, database, and graphics programs. Since the information from the electronic spreadsheet may be shared with the database manager and the word processor (and vice versa), this software is called integrated.

Intel Corporation A leading manufacturer of semiconductor devices that was founded in 1968 by Robert Noyce and Gordon Moore in Mountain View, California. In 1971, Intel engineer Marcian E. "Ted" Hoff, designed the 4-bit 4004 microprocessor chip. Throughout the years, Intel has developed a wide variety of chips and board-level products. In 1994, Intel, the world's largest producer of semiconductor ships, and Hewlett-Packard, a large computer maker, agreed to work together to develop a single chip to run in both personal computers and larger workstations. The chip should emerge by the year 2000.

interface A hardware and/or software link which enables two systems, or a computer and its peripherals, to operate as a single, integrated system. A shared boundary.

interleave To insert blank sheets between printed sheets or sets of printed sheets. Also called *slip-sheet*.

interline spacing The vertical space between lines of type, as measured from one baseline to the next. Also called *leading*.

internal hard disk A hard disk designed to fit within a computer's case and to use the computer's power supply.

internal storage Addressable storage directly controlled by the central processing unit. Used to store programs while they are being executed and data while they are being processed. Also called immediate access storage, internal memory, main storage, and primary storage. Contrast with *auxiliary storage*. See *RAM*.

International Standard Book Number The identification number assigned by a publisher for a book. See ISBN.

International Standard Serial Number An identification number assigned to magazines, newsletters, serial books and other publications. See *ISSN*.

Internet The world's largest computer network consisting of over 10,000 individual networks supporting several million computers.

introduction A section of frontmatter that, like a foreword or preface, helps set the stage for the reader of a book. The introduction often comments on the content of the book and how it should be used.

inventory Books or other publications on hand and available for sale.

inverse White letters on a black background.

invert (1) To turn over; reverse. To highlight text or objects by reversing the on-screen display or printout. For example, to invert the colors on a monochrome display means to change light to dark and dark to light. (2) To convert a logic value to its opposite, i.e., zero to one and one to zero.

invert

ISBN Acronym for International Standard Book Number, a number assigned by a publisher to individual books or publications. An ISBN is a ten-digit numeral unique to each edition or version of a book. The ISBN identifies the country of origin, publisher, and title. Libraries and book sellers use the ISBN's to ensure efficient ordering and accurate cataloging or inventory control. In the United States, the ISBN system is administered by the R.R. Bowker Company.

ISO paper sizes Printing paper sizes designated by the International Standards Organization (ISO) and used throughout the world except in the U.S. and Canada.

ISSN Acronym for International Standard Serial Number, a number assigned to magazines, newsletters, serial books and other publications. Libraries, book sellers, and news dealers rely on ISSN's to ensure efficient ordering and accurate cataloging or inventory control. In the U.S., ISSN's are assigned by the Library of Congress.

italic The slanted or cursive letterform of a typeface. True italics use a separate design and are not generated algorithmically from the Roman face.

Italic Typeface

italic

J

jacket (1) The plastic cover for a disk. It has holes and slots cut into it to expose the hub and afford the head-of-disk drive access to the disk. (2) A printed cover wrapped loosely around casebound books. Also called *dust cover*.

jaggies A term for the jagged edged formed on raster displays when displaying bitmap fonts or diagonal lines in a bitmap graphic image.

LOW-RESOLUTION   HIGH-RESOLUTION

jaggies

jargon The vocabulary peculiar to a group or profession.

jargon

jim-dash A small rule used to separate decks of a headline.

jobber A book distribution business that sells books to bookstores and libraries.

jump To continue a story from one page to another; the continuation of the story.

jumphead The title appearing above an article continued from another page.

jumpline The "continued to" line at the end of a column of text or a page which identifies the page on which an article is continued. Also known as a continued line.

justified Copy that has type flush to both the right and left. Unless text is composed of 35 or more characters per line, justified text looks awkward unless hyphenated. See *thirty-five character rule*.

JUSTIFIED	FLUSH LEFT, RAGGED RIGHT
One of the greatest scientific minds of all time, Albert Einstein is best known for his contributions to the field of physics. Born in Germany in 1879, Einstein received his diploma from the Swiss Federal Polytechnic School in Zurich, where he trained as a teacher in physics and mathematics. In 1905, he received his Ph.D. and published four research papers, the most significant being the creation of the special theory of relativity. He became internationally famous when he was awarded the Nobel Prize for Physics in 1922.	One of the greatest scientific minds of all time, Albert Einstein is best known for his contributions to the field of physics. Born in Germany in 1879, Einstein received his diploma from the Swiss Federal Polytechnic School in Zurich, where he trained as a teacher in physics and mathematics. In 1905, he received his Ph.D. and published four research papers, the most significant being the creation of the special theory of relativity. He became internationally famous when he was awarded the Nobel Prize for Physics in 1922.

justified

kerning Adjusting the space between characters to create wider or tighter spacing. Reduction of excess white space between specific letter pairs. For example, the pair To can be placed more closely together than the pair Tk because the arm of the T fits over the top of the o. Kerning is especially important with large type sizes.

kerning

kerning pairs The automatic kerning by a software application of pairs of characters which appear to be unbalanced.

keyboard Input device used to key programs and data into the computer's storage. Since the keyboard is the most frequently used part of the computer, a good keyboard is an essential part of any computer system intended for business purposes.

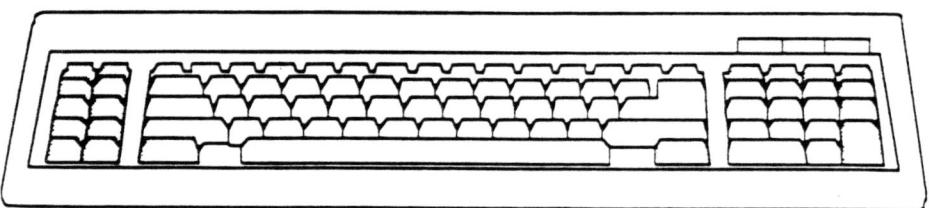

keyboard

keyboard template A plastic or cardboard card with adhesive that can be pressed onto the keyboard to explain the way a program configures the keyboard.

keyline An outline or low resolution representation of artwork to indicate size and position in the finished publication.

keystroke Action of pressing a single key or a combination of keys on a keyboard. Speed in many data entry jobs is measured in keystrokes per minute.

keyword (1) One of the significant and informative words in a title or document that describe the content of that document. (2) Set of words that have special meaning to a computer program. For example, DIR is a command that directs the operating system to produce a DIRECTORY of a disk.

kicker A small head placed above and slightly to the left of the main head.

kill (1) To terminate a process before it reaches its natural conclusion. (2) Method of erasing information. (3) To stop, frequently to abort.

kilobyte Specifically, 1024 bytes. Commonly thought of as 1000. Abbreviated K and used as a suffix when describing memory size. Thus, 24K really means a 24 x 1024 =24,576-byte memory system. Sometimes abbreviated kb.

Kromekote Trade name for a high-gloss, cast-coated paper. Commonly used for paperback book covers.

label Identifier or name used in a computer program to identify or describe an instruction statement, message, data value, record, item, or file.

label head A short descriptive headline that is used to identify a section or regular feature.

ladder An undesirable effect created when several consecutive lines end with hyphenated words.

lake A large pool of white space created by excess word spacing in unjustified type.

lamination A process of reinforcing paper with a thin, translucent or transparent film. Lamination is designed to protect the page, make it semi-permanent and add gloss. Menus and book covers are often laminated.

LAN See *local area network*.

landscape orientation An orientation in which the data has a width greater than its height. Contrast with *portrait orientation*. See *orientation*.

landscape orientation

laptop computer A personal computer, small and portable enough to be used comfortably in the lap of a person seated in an automobile or an airplane. Laptop computers are battery powered in their normal operation. Laptop computers today feature full-sized keyboards, flat-screen monitors that fold up and down, hard disks, floppy disks, and powerful microprocessors.

laptop computer

large fractions Fractions made up of text-size numbers.

large print Refers to large type for children and people with impaired vision. The text type in large print books is usually 16 points or larger.

Laser Jet A series of desktop laser printers from Hewlett-Packard Company. Introduced in 1984, it set the standard for the desktop laser printer market.

laser paper Specially prepared stock for getting as dark and as sharp an image as possible from a laser printer.

laser printer A printer that uses a light beam to transfer images to paper. Laser printers print a full page at a time. A laser is used to "paint" the dots of light onto a photographic drum or belt. The toner is applied to the drum or belt and then transferred onto the paper. In 1975, the IBM Corporation introduced the first laser printer, called the IBM 3800, which was designed for high-speed printing. In 1984, the Hewlett-Packard Company introduced the first desktop laser printer, which has revolutionized personal computer printing and has spawned desktop publishing. Desktop laser printers are technically more like an office copier than a conventional printer. They are very fast in operation and relatively silent.

laser scanner Scanner using laser beams to record images on film.

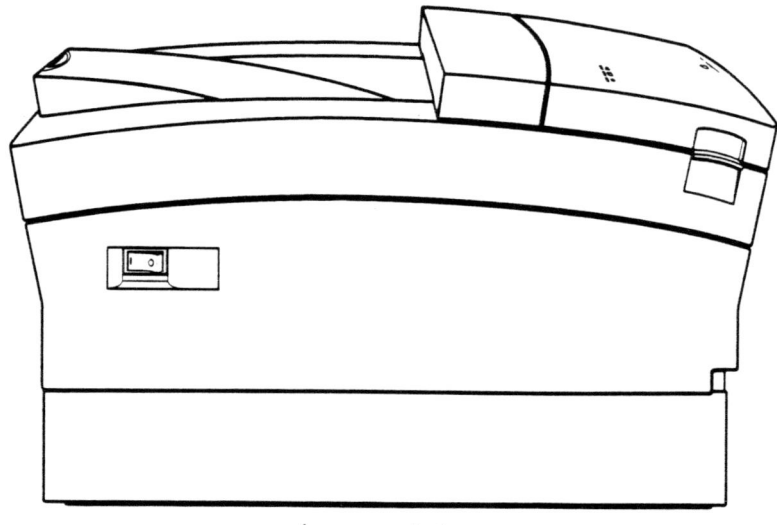
laser printer

LaserWriter A series of desktop laser printers from Apple Computer, Inc.

launch To start a program.

layer (1) In computer graphics drawing programs, an electronic overlay on which text or images can be stored. In SuperPaint, for example, you can create illustrations on two layers: a paint layer for bit-mapped graphics and a draw layer for object-oriented graphics. In some graphics programs you can draw and paint on many different layers. (2) Third dimension in a 3-D array.

layout The design or process of arranging text and graphics on a page. A layout is a working diagram of a page, with type, illustrations, and margins indicated in correct position.

lc Abbreviation for lower case.

lca Abbreviation for lower case alphabet length, used as one measure for the size of type.

LCCN See *Library of Congress Card Number*.

leader In page layout and word processing programs, a row of dots and dashes that provide a path for the eye to follow across the page. Leaders are sometimes used in table of contents to lead the reader's eye from the entry to the page number.

leading The vertical spacing between lines of type, measured from baseline to baseline. Font styles which have long ascenders and descenders need more leading than fonts that don't. In publishing, the font size and leading is described as a fraction. For example, 10/12 (which is read "10 on 12") indicates 10 point type with 2 point leading. Pronounced "ledding."

26 POINTS
BASELINE TO BASELINE

Leading is the space between lines of type

24-POINT TYPE WITH 2 POINTS LEADING

leading

leading edge (1) In optical scanning, the edge of the document or page that enters the read position first. (2) Buzz word implying technological leadership: "on the leading edge of technology."

leaf One sheet of paper in a publication; each side of a leaf is one page.

leaflet Small poster or advertising handout; a single-page, single-sided publication.

left justification A method of aligning text so that each line of text is flush against the left margin, leaving a ragged or uneven right margin.

left opener A book chapter which begins on a verso (left-facing) page.

legal size page A page designed to be printed on 8.5- by 14-inch paper.

legend (1) Text beneath a graph; it explains the colors, shading, or symbols used to label the data points. (2) Text that describes or explains an illustration, photograph or other image.

legibility Refers to the ease or difficulty with which type is perceived. Legibility is affected by type size and style, leading, and line length; it is a property of the letter's design.

letter elements The calligraphic design elements that comprise the identity of individual characters. See *apex, arc, arm, bar, beak, crossbar, spine, stem, tail* and *vortex*.

letter fit The overall looseness or tightness of how the letters of a font fit together on a line, with no tracking, kerning, or letterspacing.

letterform The design shape of a letter of the alphabet.

letter quality printing High-quality output produced by some printers. Laser printers, daisy-wheel printers and ink-jet printers are letter quality printers. High-end, 24-pin dot matrix printers provide near letter quality printing.

letter size page A page that is 8.5- by 11-inches in size.

letterspacing can be adjusted   NORMAL LETTERSPACING

letterspacing can be adjusted   INCREASED LETTERSPACING

letterspacing

letterspacing Extra space or air inserted between letters or words on a line. Most desktop publishing systems and typesetters can reduce or increase letterspacing in uniform increments. In positive letterspacing, space is added between letters in the same increment. In negative letterspacing, space is subtracted from between letters in the same increment.

library (1) Published collection of programs, routines, and subroutines available to every user of the computer. (2) A storage area, usually on hard disk or a diskette, used to store programs. (3) A collection of items, such as clip art, intended for inclusion in other programs. (4) A collection of books.

Library of Congress The library of the United States Congress, in Washington, D.C., which is, de facto, the national library of the U.S. It is the deposit library for books printed and published in the U.S.

Library of Congress Card Number A number assigned to a book to help catalog it for storage and retrieval in a library. See *CIP*.

ligated A typeface that has connections between letters.

ligature

ligature One character that is made up of two or more letters. Ligatures are unnecessary in photosetting where there is no type, but are sometimes retained for aesthetic reasons.

light In typesetting, type that is designed with much thinner strokes than the regular face of that type family.

lightface A typefont less bold than a Roman font of the same family; extra light version of a typeface. Compare *boldface*.

lightness How light or dark an image is.

light pen Electronic input device that resembles a pen and can be used to write or sketch on the screen of a graphics display.

line art

line art Artwork containing only blacks and whites with no shading. Line art can be reproduced accurately by low to medium resolution printers.

line break The blank line that separates two paragraphs.

line feed (LF) Operation that advances printer paper by one line.

line graph Graph made by connecting data points with a line. Shows the variations of data over time or the relationships between two numeric variables.

line length The length of a line of type; the area between two margins.

line printer A printer that assembles all characters on a line at one time and prints them out practically simultaneously. Line printers are high-speed printing devices that are usually connected to mainframes and minicomputers.

line screen In reference to halftones — the screen frequency, resolution or dots per inch of a screen. An 80 dot-per-inch screen is called an 80 line screen.

line spacing The space between lines of text. The distance from baseline to baseline between two lines of type. See *leading*.

line style The designation of a style of a rule, such as solid, dashed, etc.

line up When two lines of type, or a line of type and illustration, align to the same imaginary horizontal or vertical line.

line weight The thickness of a single line of a font character. Also called *stroke weight*.

lining figures Digits which are all base-aligned with accompanying text.

linotype A machine that made printing letters by casting characters line by line was built by Ottmar Mergenthaler (U.S.) in 1886. Mergenthaler's machine was built on an order placed by the editor of the *New York Herald Tribune*.

liquid crystal display (LCD) A flat display used in many portable computers because it is small, and requires little power. The display is made of two sheets of polarizing material sandwiched together with a nematic liquid crystal solution between them. Images are produced when electric currents cause the liquid crystals to align so light cannot shine through.

liquid laminate Plastic applied as a liquid to paper, then bonded and cured into a hard glossy finish. See *UV coating*.

literary agent A businessperson who acts as an intermediary between author and publisher, advising on manuscripts and negotiating terms. The agent's fee is normally 10 percent of royalties, paid by the author.

Literary Market Place (LMP) The bible of book professionals, this guide has long served as the single most frequently consulted source of publishers throughout the U.S. publishing industry. The LMP is updated annually and is published by the R.R. Bowker Company.

lithography Another name for offset printing, which is a reproduction process in which sheets or continuous webs of material are printed by impressing them with images from ink applied to a rubber blanket on a rotating cylinder from a metal or plastic plate attached to another cylinder. Lithography was invented in 1796 by the German typographer Aloys Senefelder. He realized that a drawing done with a soft-lead pencil on limestone (the word lithography comes from the Greek *lithos*, meaning stone) is water resistant. However, the unmarked stone absorbs water. If a coat of greasy ink is spread over the surface of the stone, it will not stick to the wet spots, only to the greased areas. The stone has therefore only to be placed in the press and it reproduces the initial drawing. Senefelder rapidly improved his method. Instead of water, he used a solution of gum-arabic and nitric acid, which is completely impervious to printer's ink.

line area The imaging area within which an output device can place a character or graphic element.

line matter Typeset material preserved for later use.

LMP See *Literary Market Place*.

load (1) To read information into the storage of a computer. (2) To put a diskette into a disk drive. (3) To insert paper into a printer.

local area network (LAN) A privately run communications network of several machines located within a mile or so of one another.

logo See *logotype*.

log off To terminate connection with the computer.

log on Action by which a user begins a terminal session.

logotype Character(s) designed as a company logo or trademark.

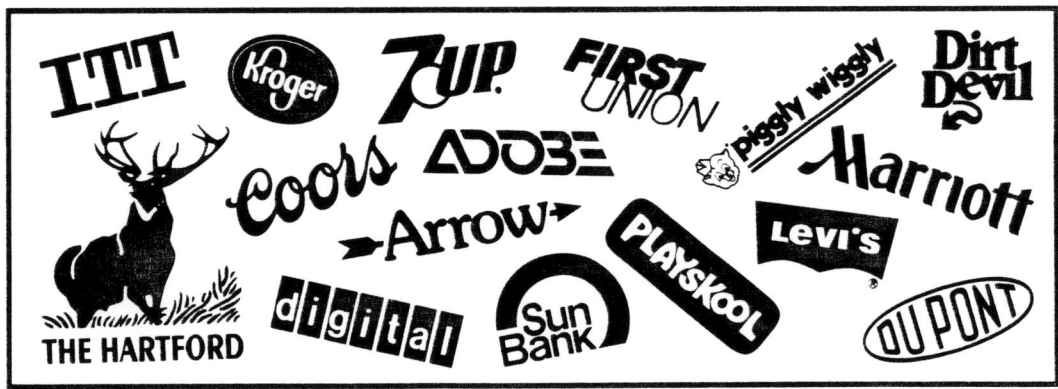

logotype

loose leaf binding A type of binding in which pages have three holes punched or drilled through them. Pages are held together by metal or plastic fasteners or they are inserted in three ring notebooks.

loose line A line in justified text containing excess word spacing.

low end Computer jargon for an inexpensive product, from the bottom of a company's product list.

lower case The small letters of the alphabet. Indicated as LC.

abcdefghijklmnop

lower case

low-resolution Pertaining to the quality and accuracy of detail that can be represented by a graphics display. Resolution quality depends upon the number of basic image-forming units (pixels) within a picture image — the greater the number, the higher the resolution. Low-resolution pictures, produced by a small number of pixels, are not as sharp and clear as high-resolution pictures.

lpi Acronym for lines per inch, the number of possible halftone spots that can occur in a square inch.

Macintosh A series of popular microcomputers from Apple Computer, Inc. first introduced in 1984. It uses the Motorola 68000 family of microprocessors and the Power PC chip, and a proprietary operating system that simulates a user's desktop on screen. This standard user interface, combined with its built-in QuickDraw graphics language, has provided a visual, easy-to-use microcomputer. The Macintosh uses a mouse as a primary input device, in addition to a keyboard. Since the introduction of the Macintosh, Apple Computer, Inc. continues to offer progressively faster and more powerful models of the Macintosh.

magazines Periodicals published at intervals varying from weekly to quarterly.

magnetic media Generic name for floppy disks, tapes, and any other devices that store data in the form of magnetic impulses.

magnify (1) To enlarge an area of the screen, usually for editing purposes. (2) The process of algorithmically enlarging a given font or character.

mainframe Large, expensive computer generally used for information processing in large businesses, colleges, and organizations. Originally, the phrase referred to the extensive array of large rack and panel cabinets that held thousands of vacuum tubes in early computers. Mainframes can occupy an entire room and have very large data-handling capacities. Far more costly than microcomputers or minicomputers, mainframes are the largest, fastest, and most expensive class of computers. Supercomputers are the largest, fastest, and most expensive of the mainframes. Before minicomputers became popular in 1965, all computers were mainframes.

Mainz Psalter The first dated printed book completed, according to the colophon, on August 14, 1457. It was printed by Fust and Schoeffer at Mainz using the materials and equipment which they had taken over from Gutenberg. It is a book intended to imitate the manuscript, Psalters, then in use for liturgical purposes.

makeready Copy or machine preparation of graphic material before production.

makeup Placing elements on a page, whether by hand or by computer.

Maltron keyboard An alternate keyboard layout that allows potentially much faster speeds, and is easier to learn than the traditional QWERTY keyboard layout. See *Dvorak keyboard* and *QWERTY keyboard.*

manuscript The original handwritten, typewritten copy, or computer printed copy from which typeset copy will be produced.

marbled paper Decorated paper used for book endpapers. The decoration resembles the patterns to be found in marble, from which the name is derived.

margin White space surrounding the text or picture area on a page; the area of the page that is left blank. The four margins of a page are gutter, head margin (also top margin), outside margin, and bottom margin.

mark up copy A copy that contains information needed by the typesetter or desktop computer operator: typeface, size, style, line length, leading, etc.

marquee A rectangular area surrounded by dotted lines used to select objects or selected portions of an image in a drawing/painting program.

mass market paperback A soft cover book of standard size (4 3/16- by 6 3/4-inch) distribution through wholesalers and jobbers to various types of booksellers. Mass market books are sold in newsstands, airports, drugstores, discount stores, etc., rather than just bookstores.

master page A page in which the user can store the layout elements that repeat in all the pages in a publication.

masthead A logo or design that identifies a newsletter, newspaper, or magazine.

mathematical signs Typographic symbols such as + (plus), - (minus), x (multiplication), ÷ (division), = (equals) and > (greater than). Symbols used in mathematical formulas.

matte finish Flat (non-glossy) finish on coated printing paper.

maximize To zoom or enlarge a window so that it fills the display screen.

mean line The top (imaginary) point of all lowercase characters without ascenders. Also called "x-height."

measure The length of a typeset line, expressed in picas and points. Also *line length* and *column width*.

mechanical Camera-ready copy with text and art already in position for photographing or copying. A mechanical is the final arrangement of type and images that will appear on the printed page.

mechanical binding Bindings using wire, staples or plastic.

mechanical pencil The first automatic mechanical pencil, called the Ever-Sharp Pencil, was invented in 1915 by Rokuji Hayakawa (Japan), founder in 1912 of a company to which the mechanical pencil gave its name. The Sharp Corporation has since broadened its activities, particularly in electronics, copy machines, computer scanners, and laser printers.

media (1) The plural of medium. All forms of computer storage methods such as disks, film and paper. (2) All forms of publication, such as books, magazines, newsletters and broadcast publishing via TV and radio.

medium A means of conveying information; any physical substance upon which data are recorded, such as magnetic disk, magnetic tape, CD-ROM, film and paper.

megabyte One million or 1,049,576 bytes or characters. It is also written as MB, Mb, Mbyte, M-byte and met.

megahertz (MHZ) A speed measurement for computer processors, describing the clock speed or operational cycle of the central processing unit (CPU).

memory Storage facilities of the computer, capable of storing vast amounts of data. See *floppy disk, hard disk* and *random access memory (RAM)*.

memory address A name, letter or number that identifies a specific location where information is stored in a computer's memory.

memory chip A semiconductor device used to store information in the form of electrical charges. There are two types of memory chips: ROM holds information permanently while RAM holds it temporarily. Memory is often added to a computer simply by plugging RAM chips into sockets.

menu A list of command options available to the user of computer software program. An on-screen list of command choices.

menu bar A horizontal menu at the top of a display screen or window. See *pull-down menu*.

metaphor In software development, the use of words or pictures to suggest a resemblance. For example the Apple Macintosh computer uses a desk-top metaphor with its icons for paper, files, folders, wastebaskets, and so on.

metrics Font information such as ascent, descent, leading, character widths, and kerning.

metric system Decimal measurement; the basic unit for designers is the millimeter (mm) and centimeter (cm). One centimeter = 0.3937 inch; one millimeter = 0.0394 inch.

mickey A unit of mouse movement typically set at 1/200th of an inch.

microcomputer

microcomputer The smallest and least expensive class of computer. Any small computer that uses a microprocessor as its central processing unit (CPU). The terms microcomputer and personal computer are synonymous.

microfloppy disk A 3.5-inch floppy disk, which in recent years has become the disk of choice. A 3.5-inch disk holds more data and are much easier to store, transport and handle than their 5.25-inch counterparts. The microfloppy disk was developed by Sony.

microprocessor The complex chip that is the central processing unit (CPU) of the computer. The job of the microprocessor is to control what goes on inside the computer. All processing that a computer does takes place in the microprocessor. Following court proceedings lasting 20 years, the U.S. Patent Office, on July 17, 1990 recognized Gilbert Hyatt as the inventor of the microprocessor. His patent, deposited in December 1970, was the first to refer to a unique integrated circuit that contained all the necessary elements for the computer. Prior to the court's decision, the invention had been attributed to Marcian E. Hoff, Federico Faggin and Stanley Mazor of Intel Corporation. These engineers did create the first commercial microchip in history in 1971 — the Intel 4004 — however their patents were related to particular aspects of the invention, but not to its general concept.

Microsoft Corporation A leading software company founded in 1975 by William H. Gates and Paul G. Allen. The companies first product was Microsoft BASIC for the Altair 8800 microcomputer. Following products include MS-DOS, Microsoft Windows, Microsoft Word, Microsoft Works, Microsoft Excel, GW-BASIC, QBASIC, QuickBASIC, Visual BASIC, as well as many other software systems. Microsoft's position as the supplier of the major software to the world's largest computer base (IBM-compatible microcomputers) gives it considerable influence over the future of the computer industry.

Microsoft Windows A graphics-based operating environment for IBM-compatible microcomputers from Microsoft Corporation. It runs in conjunction with DOS. Some of the graphical user interface features include pull-down menus, multiple typefaces, desk accessories, and the capability of moving text and graphics from one program to another via a clipboard.

Microsoft Word A full-featured word processing program for IBM-compatible microcomputers and Apple Macintosh computers from Microsoft Corporation. It has a spelling checker, hyphenation, style sheets, a glossary, mail merge, automatic text wrap, and a column design feature.

minicomputer A class of computers with capabilities and a price between microcomputers and mainframes.

minifloppy A 5.25-inch diskette, introduced by Shugart in 1978.

minus leading Leading in which the baseline to baseline space is less than the point size or less than solid, i.e., 18/16. Used primarily to tighten up and improve the appearance of headlines.

minus letterspacing Reduction of the normal space allocated between characters.

misprint A typographical error once it is printed.

mixing The practice of using more than one size or style of type in a line or block of copy.

mockup Same as *dummy*.

model release A form giving permission to use a photograph of an individual for publication.

modem Acronym for MOdulator/DEModulator, a device that translates digital pulses from a computer into analog signals for telephone transmission, and analog signals from the telephone into digital pulses the computer can understand. Provides communication capabilities between computer equipment over common telephone facilities.

modern A modified version of Old Style, these high contrast letters have heavy, untapered stems and light serifs.

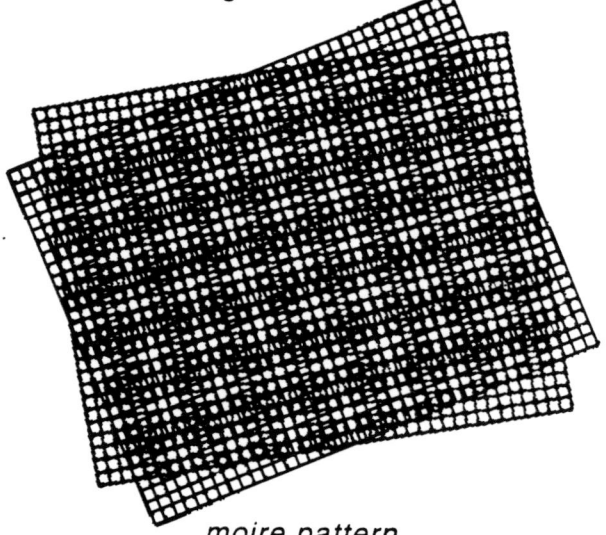

moire pattern

moire pattern The undesired effect caused by overlaying dot patterns (usually halftone representation of photographs) which are incompatible. Pronounced mor-ray.

monitor

monitor (1) A device on which images generated by the computer's video adapter are displayed. (2) Control program or supervisor.

monochrome display A video display capable of displaying only one color. It generally has a higher resolution than a color monitor and is often more suitable for word processing and information processing use, which require long periods of user viewing.

monofont A font in which each character occupies the same horizontal width as any other. See *proportional font*.

monospaced type Like typewritten characters, monospaced type has the same width and take up the same amount of space. Use of this type allows figures to be set in vertical rows without leaving a ragged appearance (as opposed to proportional type).

monotype In 1887 Tolbert Lanston (U.S.) invented a machine that could cast and typeset individual characters from hot metal. It permitted the typesetting of 9,000 characters per hour.

morphing A special graphics effect that makes it look like one image is transformed into another image.

Motorola, Inc. A leading manufacturer of semiconductor devices. Although the company produces many consumer electronics products, they are best known in the computer business as the manufacturer of the 68000 family of microprocessors.

mouse A hand-operated pointing device that senses movements as it is moved across a flat surface and conveys this information to the computer. The mouse also has one or more buttons that can be pressed to signal the computer. The mouse's main advantage is that it can move a cursor around on the display screen, including, diagonally, with great precision. See *mechanical mouse* and *optical mouse*.

mouse

mouse pad A surface to be used with a mouse. As you move the mouse across the mouse pad, the cursor moves across the screen in the same direction. The mouse pad is made from foam rubber that makes it easy to roll the ball in the mouse.

mouse pointer The on-screen icon or cursor, the movement of which is controlled by the mouse.

movable characters The first movable characters were made of clay. A Chinese invention, the first known movable type machine was built by Bi Sheng in 1041.

ms Abbreviation for manuscript.

MS-DOS Acronym for Microsoft-Disk Operating System, the standard operating system for IBM compatible microcomputers. MS-DOS was created by Microsoft Corporation and released in 1981. MS-DOS oversees such operations as disk input and output, video support, keyboard control, and many internal functions related to program execution and file maintenance.

multicolor printing Printing with more than one color. Normally, multicolor printing uses two, three, or four colors. Many children's books are printed in two or three colors, as this is less expensive than four colors.

multiple master typeface A font technology, created by Adobe Systems as an extension of its PostScript Type 1 font format, that turns one typeface into a whole type family. Instead of a single typeface design, a multiple master typeface is a design matrix made up of one or more of the variables of weight, width, size, and style. The typeface can be modified along any of these axes while still keeping the essential characteristics of the typeface.

NADTP Acronym for National Association of Desktop Publishers, an organization with active members from all sectors of the computer publishing industry. NADTP provides its members with a wide variety of informational services.

naked column A column of text without a headline or art at the top.

nameplate The title at the top of a newsletter, which may also contain a logo, a tagline, and the volume number. Also called a *flag* or *masthead*.

nanosecond A billionth of a second. Used to measure the speed of logic and memory chips. Light travels approximately one foot per nanosecond.

narrow type A typeface that is algorithmically generated to achieve the look of a condensed font. For example, Helvetica Narrow is derived by compressing the regular Helvetica family in the x-direction by a scale factor of 0.75.

National Association of Desktop Publishers (NADTP) A trade organization for desktop publishing professionals.

near letter quality (NLQ) A printer whose output is almost as good as an electric typewriter.

negative Any image on paper or film where dark elements appear light and light elements appear dark; reverse photographic image. See *positive*.

negative italic The displayed attribute of leaning upward to the left. See *positive italic*.

network (1) When two or more computers are connected to allow them to share the same software and information. Used primarily in businesses and schools. (2) System of interconnected computer systems and terminals. (3) Structure of relationships among a project's activities, tasks, and events. (4) A means of organizing data in artificial intelligence systems. A type of knowledge representation in artificial intelligence. (5) A system of computers, and often peripherals such as printers and scanners, linked together. See *bus network, ring network* and *star network*.

neutral gray Any level of gray from white to black with no apparent color cast or hue.

neutral pH paper See *acid free paper*.

newsletter A coverless periodical that generally contains no advertising.

newspapers A newspaper is usually defined as a serial publication issued at regular intervals between daily and weekly, whose primary function is to carry stories about current events. The first gazette to come out regularly appeared in Antwerp, Belgium in 1605. It was widely imitated in Europe and, from 1609, two weekly gazettes appeared in Germany. The first daily newspaper was published by Thimotheus Ritzch in Leipzig, Germany.

newsprint Paper used for printing newspapers.

news release An announcement sent by a book publisher to newspapers and magazines and other businesses to draw publicity for new books. Also called *press release*.

NiCad battery pack An abbreviation for Nickel Cadmium, a battery pack used for many portable computers.

non-breaking space Space inserted between two related words to ensure that they appear together on the same line.

nonimpact printer Printer that uses electricity, heat, laser technology, ink jets, or photographic techniques to print output. A printer that prints without striking the paper. Contrast with *impact printer*.

nonproportional Refers to the spacing between characters of an entire font set. See *monospaced type*.

normal space width A setting that determines normal word spacing in unjustified lines of text.

Norton Utilities A package of utility programs for IBM-compatible microcomputers, including a benchmark program that measures a computer's throughput, an undelete program that restores files accidently deleted from the disk, management utilities for directories and subdirectories, and data security programs.

novelty type A group of type styles whose designs create a mood or impression.

numeric keypad A separate section of the keyboard that contains keys for typing numbers. The keypad contains the digits 0 to 9 and a decimal point key.

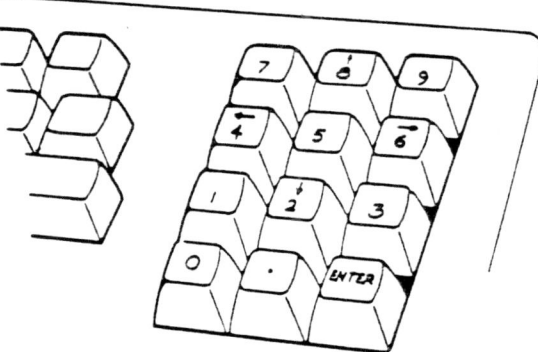

numeric keypad

numbering Most word processing and page layout programs offer automatic page numbering.

object-oriented graphics Computer graphics that are based on the use of "construction elements" such as curves, lines, and squares. Object-oriented graphics describe an image mathematically as a set of instructions for creating the objects in the image. Object-oriented graphics enable the user to manipulate objects as entire units. Because objects are described mathematically, object-oriented graphics can also be rotated, magnified and layered relatively easily. Object-oriented graphics can usually be displayed or printed at the full resolution of the monitor or output device, offering more precision than bit-mapped images.

object-oriented graphics

oblique See *italic*.

oblique axis An axis that is placed at an angle to the margins of a page.

oblique type A typeface that has upright strokes at an angle to the vertical axis. In contrast to true italic typefaces that are designed, oblique typefaces are algorithmically generated from the Roman typeface.

offline Pertaining to equipment, devices, or persons not in direct communication with the central processing unit of a computer. Equipment not connected to the computer. Contrast with *online*.

offset indent See *hand indent*.

offset printing The predominant commercial printing process in which mechanicals are photographed and converted into flexible printing plates that transfer the document image to paper. Offset printing produces excellent results quickly while using inexpensive materials and processes. Offset printing was invented by lithographer W. Rubel (U.S.) in 1904. The word offset covers the same transfer technique as lithography. See *lithography*.

old style A family of typefaces characterized by wide round letters, fairly even stroke widths, and sloping serifs. Garamond, Baskerville and Caslon are examples. Old style type designs were developed during the late 15th century through the middle of the 18th century.

omnifont The ability of an optical character reader to recognize any typeface font without having to "learn" that typeface. Omnifont character recognition uses feature extraction techniques.

one-color printing The reproduction of an image in a single color, whether red, blue, brown, green, some other hue, or black.

on-line information service A service that allows you to use your computer to do a variety of activities such as shopping, making travel reservations, buying and selling stocks, sending and receiving electronic mail, accessing an encyclopedia, and other information related activities.

on-screen help Operating assistance for applications that appear directly on the monitor, saving you the bother of looking them up in a manual.

on-screen layout Sometimes known as an electronic pasteup, it is the method used to prepare a document using computer software to position all elements on the page. The finished layout, containing text and illustrations, is then output on a printer and is ready for copying or reproduction.

on-screen pasteup A layout on a computer monitor.

opacity Characteristic of paper that prevents printing on one side from showing through to the other.

opaque ink In printing, ink that blocks out the underlying ink.

open matter Type set with abundant line spacing or containing many short lines.

operating system (OS) The master set of programs that manage the computer. Among other things, an operating system controls input and output to and from the keyboard, screen, disks, and other peripheral devices; loads and begins the execution of other programs; manages the storage of data on disks; and provides scheduling and accounting services. The OS is a master control program that runs the computer and acts as a scheduler and traffic cop. See *MS-DOS, OS-2, System 7,* and *UNIX.*

optical character recognition (OCR) Information processing technology that converts human-readable data in a special OCR font into another medium for computer input. Light reflected from characters is recognized by OCR equipment. The process by which text on paper is scanned and converted into text files in a computer.

optical disk A large capacity storage device. Several types of optical disks are available: CD-ROM (compact disk, read-only memory), WORM (write once, read many) and erasable optical disk drives that let you write data as well as read it. Erasable optical disks are impervious to magnetic fields and can hold data for many years. This storage technology uses a laser beam to store large amounts of data at relatively low cost.

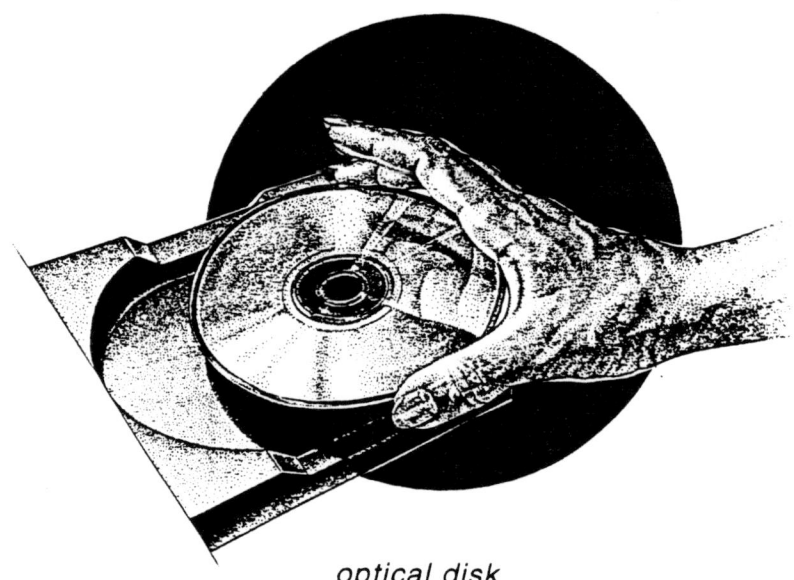

optical disk

optical scaling Subtly adjusting the design of a typeface from size to size, to improve readability.

optical scanner An input device that reads into the computer characters and images that are printed on a paper form.

optima Designed by Hermann Zapf in 1958, Optima is a widely used typeface in Europe and the U.S.

optimum format A design that uses body type at or near the optimum line length.

orientation Screen displays and printer output may appear in either of two orientations: landscape or portrait. With landscape orientation, the page is wider than it is long; with portrait orientation, the page is longer than it is wide. See *landscape orientation* and *portrait orientation.*

original The original material to be used for reproduction.

ornamental borders Decorative borders. Often ornamental borders were made up of pieces of type, with special characters designed for corners. These were called combination ornaments, and can be made on the computer with illustration tools.

ornaments Characters that are not letters but decorative typographic elements, which can be used alone or combined into borders or other patterns. See *dingbats.*

ornaments

orphan A word or short line ending a paragraph which carried over to the top of the next column.

OS (1) Acronym for Operating System. A group of programs that control a computer and make it possible for users to enter and run their own programs. Some examples of OS are: MS-DOS, OS/2, System 7 and UNIX. (2) Abbreviation for Old Style type, typefaces with ascenders and descenders.

OS/2 A microcomputer operating system from the IBM Corporation that allows multitasking by a single user. OS/2 was introduced in 1987. Several important OS/2 subsystems include Presentation Manager, which provides a graphical user interface, and LAN Manager, which provides networking facilities. OS/2 is designed for use on microcomputers based on Intel 80x86 processors: 80286, 80386 and 80486 and Pentium.

Otabind A binding process for paperback books that resembles perfect binding but allows a book to be opened out flat.

outdent A paragraph style in which the first line of a paragraph is set flush with the left margin and all subsequent lines are indented. See *hanging indent.*

outline font A font that is defined by drawing the black contour of the white space that makes up each character. It is made up typically of Bezier curves for PostScript fonts and quadratic splines for TrueType fonts. Both of these fonts can be scaled to any size; therefore, one set of outlines can be used for any size in a typeface.

ABCDEFGHIJKLMNOPQRSTUV
ABCDEFGHIJKLMNOPQR

outline font

out of print Publication that a publisher no longer has available and does not plan to reprint.

output device Unit used for taking out data values from a computer and presenting them in the desired form to the user, such as a printer or display screen.

output device

outriggers Horizontal rules that set off blocks of text. See *rule*.

outside margin The right margin of a right-hand page or the left margin of a left-hand page; the outer, vertical edge of a page, opposite the binding edge.

overage Copies printed in excess of specified quantities. Also called overrun.

overlapping Typesetting letters partially over one another.

overlay A part of an image that is formed by laying multiple images, one upon the other.

overline

overline   Descriptive type placed above a picture or graphic element.

overprint   To print one image over a previously printed image, such as printing type or a graphic image over a screen tint.

overrun   The quantity of printed copies over and above the number ordered to be printed.

overscore   A thin line placed above individual characters. Opposite of an underline.

overset   A typeset line that exceeds a given line length.

oversize books   Books that in physical dimensions are larger than normal (i.e., 10 to 12 inches tall or over).

overstriking   Ability of a hard-copy printer to strike a character more than once to produce special effects: boldface characters, character with a line through it, etc.

oxford rule   A border made up of heavy and light rules in parallel pairs.

packaged software Software that is packaged and sold in stores and by mail order. The prepared package consists of the program on diskette(s), operating manual and possibly other documentation.

padding Space added around the outside of the perimeter of a frame to prevent it from abutting text.

page Amount of text or graphic material displayed on a screen at one time.

page break (1) The location where one page ends and another begins. (2) A special code placed in a document to mark the end of a page.

page composition software Software that lets users compose pages merging graphic images (such as illustrations, scanned photos, line art, diagrams and charts) and text imported from a word processing program or created inside the page composition program itself. Page composition software is the heart of the desktop publishing system. It gives users the power to electronically cut, paste and layout pages. Users can define margins and rules, kern letters, position text and graphics on the page, flow text from one column or page to another column or page and specify hyphenation and justification, among other functions.

page description language (PDL) A programming language with specialized instructions for describing how to print a whole page. If an application generates output in a page description language, the output can be printed on any printer that supports it.

page design The process of specifying the boundaries of text or graphics on a page. Includes choosing margins, page length, headings and footings.

page layout program In desktop publishing, an application program that assembles text and graphics from a variety of files, with which you can determine the precise placement, scaling, sizing, and cropping of material in accordance with the page design represented on-screen. Popular page layout programs are *PageMaker, Quark XPress,* and *Ventura Publisher.*

PageMaker See *Aldus PageMaker*.

page orientation See *orientation*.

page preview A mode found on many page layout and word processing programs that shows a full-page view of how a page will look when printed out, including added elements such as headers, footers, and margins.

page printer A printer that prints an entire page at a time rather than letter by letter.

page printer

page proofs The secondary stage in the proofing process in which pages have been paginated.

page size The actual dimensions of a document. They may differ from paper size.

pages per inch (ppi) A term used to measure the thickness of paper stock.

page view The degree of magnification of page on a monitor screen.

pagination (1) The integration of text, illustrations and pictures into a whole page. (2) Process of numbering or ordering pages. (3) The dividing of a document into pages.

paint program A program for creating and manipulating pixel images, as opposed to creating and manipulating object-oriented graphics. A paint program, because it treats a drawing as a group of dots (pixels), is particularly appropriate for freehand drawing. Paint programs create raster graphics images.

palatino Hermann Zapf designed palatino in 1950, and it rapidly became one of the most used types in the world. Zapf participated in the digitization of palatino, thus, one of the great typefaces is available in desktop publishing in a version approved by its designer.

AaBbCcDdEeFfGgHhIiJjKkLlMmNn

palatino

palette (1) Set of available colors or patterns in a computer graphics system. (2) In a paint program, a collection of drawing tools, such as patterns, colors, different line widths, brush shapes, from which the user can choose.

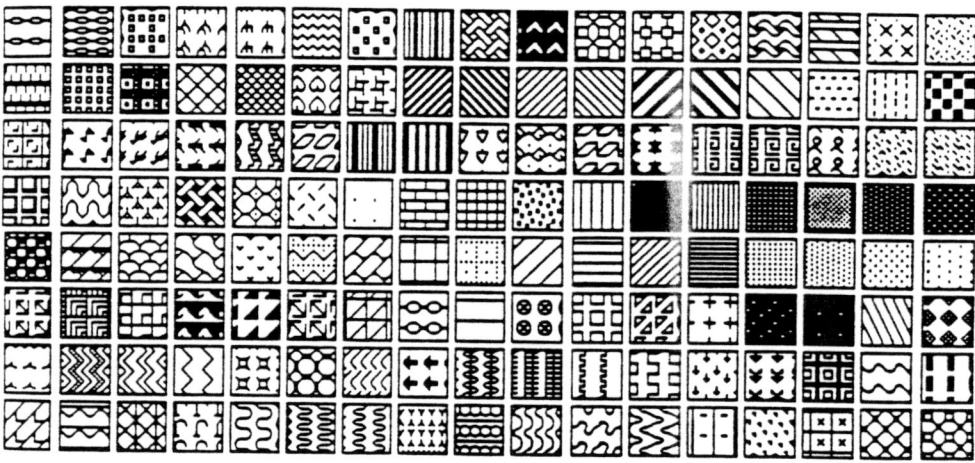

palette

pamphlet A publication of a few pages, often folded and saddle-stapled. See *booklet*.

panning Moving a graphic image horizontally or vertically inside its frame in order to see those parts beyond its frame.

Pantone Matching System (PMS) Specific ink color specifications widely used in printing and color graphics. An extensive catalog of Pantone colors are available which describe about 500 colors; each assigned a unique PMS number. The Pantone color-selection system is supported by a variety of high-end illustration programs. A color system standardized by the Pantone Corporation.

paper The word "paper" comes from Egypt's papyrus stalk, a tall reed used for writing material as long ago as 3000 B.C. The tall reeds, which grew along the Nile River to heights of 19 feet, were cultivated in Egypt and their various parts used not only as writing material, but also for food, and for the making of loincloths, sails, boats, baskets, ropes, and sandals. Actual papermaking did not begin until 105 A.D. in China, where an official of the Imperial court created paper sheets using mulberry and other plant fibers. The techniques rapidly improved, and paper reached neighboring countries first (Vietnam, Korea and Japan), and then Arab countries in the 8th century. It was the Arabs who introduced paper to Europe when they brought it to Spain. The Silos missal, from near Burgos in Spain, is the oldest manuscript on European paper. It dates back to the beginning of the 11th century. The making of book paper from wood pulp originated around 1800. In 1799 Nicholas Robert, employed in Paris at the Francois Didot Bookshop and Printers , obtained a patent "for the manufacture of an extraordinary paper, measuring between 39 ft. and 49 ft. long, without the need for any workman and by purely mechanical means." This invention was improved by Bryan Donkin (Great Britain) in 1803. It enabled the paper mill to free itself from the traditional method of manufacturing paper — sheet by sheet in a tank.

paperback A book bound with a flexible paper cover. See *perfect binding*.

paper size The dimensions of a sheet of paper that can be used by a computer printer. Standard paper sizes are letter (8.5 by 11 inches), legal (8.5 by 14 inches), 11 by 17 inches. European A4 (8.27 by 11.69 inches) and B5 (6.93 by 9.84 inches).

papyrus Writing material used in the ancient world. Papyrus is the dried leaves of papyrus grass, a reed which grows in profusion along the banks of the River Nile. The Egyptians are usually credited with the invention of papyrus around 3000 B.C.

paragraph mark A symbol indicating a paragraph.

paragraphs Units of English composition.

parallel printer Printer that receives information from the computer one character (letter, number, etc.) at a time through eight wires. Additional wires are used to exchange control signals. A parallel printer is designed to be connected to the computer's parallel port.

parchment An early writing medium created from the skins of animals, usually that of a sheep or a goat. It was, no doubt, the commercial and cultural rivalry between the Pharoh Ptolemy and the King of Pergamum in Asia Minor which, between 196 and 156 B.C., brought about the invention of parchment. The pharoah, taking umbrage at the growing reputation of Pergamum as a cultural center, must have stopped providing it with papyrus, thus obliging the scribes of Pergamum to invent a new material.

parenthesis Punctuation mark, ( ). Often used to enclose supplementary text.

parity bit Extra bit added to a byte, character, or word to ensure that there is always either an even number or an odd number of bits, according to the logic of the system. If through a hardware failure, a bit should be lost in transmission, its loss can be detected by checking the parity.

park To position a hard drive's read/write head so that the drive is not damaged while being transported.

partitioning (1) Subdividing a computer storage area into smaller units allocated to specific jobs or tasks. (2) Breaking up a problem into subtasks.

password Special word, code, or symbol that must be presented to the computer system to gain access to its resources. Used for identification and security purposes on a computer system.

paste To place information previously cut from a document into a new position. With some computer systems, areas of text or graphics may be cut from a document, saved, and later pasted into another document. See *cut-and-paste*.

paste up The preparation of a mechanical; traditional method of laying out a page of camera ready work. Literally cutting and pasting.

pattern Any arrangement of lines, dots or symbols used fill a graphic object.

payment on acceptance The author is paid for his or her work as soon as the publisher decides to use it.

payment on publication The author is paid for his or her work when it is published.

PC Acronym for Personal Computer. Often means an IBM compatible microcomputer.

PC compatibility Refers to a microcomputer that is compatible in some way with the popular IBM Personal Computer and IBM Personal System/2. Many levels of compatibility are possible.

PC-DOS Acronym for Personal Computer-Disk Operating System. IBM Corporation's trade name for its version of MS-DOS, an operating system developed and licensed by Microsoft Corporation for computers that use Intel Corporation microprocessors. There is effectively no difference between PC-DOS and MS-DOS.

PCL Acronym for Printer Command Language, a Hewlett-Packard language used and supported by their laser printers.

PC Tools A software package of file and disk management utility programs for Apple Macintosh computers and IBM personal computers and compatibles.

PDL Acronym for Page Description Language, a generic term referring to a language used for creating text and graphics within a printer. PostScript and QuickDraw are page description languages.

PE Abbreviation for Printer's Error.

pencil In 1564 the discovery of graphite in Cumbria, England led to the invention of lead pencils. In 1792, the engineer Jacques Nicolas Conte (France) invented graphite and clay pencils covered with cedar wood. Demand crossed international borders, and his pencils were soon to reach all parts of the world.

percent The symbol representing percentage (%).

perfect binding A binding process that employs the use of a flexible adhesive to hold the pages together. The pages held tightly together are bound off, and an adhesive is applied to this area, and a wraparound cover applied while the adhesive is still wet. Perfect binding creates the common paperback book.

perfect binding

periodical A publication issued on a regular schedule, such as every month. Magazines, journals and newsletters are periodicals.

peripheral equipment Input/output units and auxiliary storage units of a computer system, attached by cables to the central processing unit. Used to get data in and data out, and to act as a reservoir for large amounts of data that cannot be held in the central processing unit at one time. The laser printer, hard disk and optical scanner are examples of peripherals.

permanent font A font which is downloaded to the printer, onto a hard disk, or in ROM, and resides there until the power is turned off.

personal computer (PC) The smallest and least expensive class of computer. A computer designed for use by one person at a time. Also called a *microcomputer*.

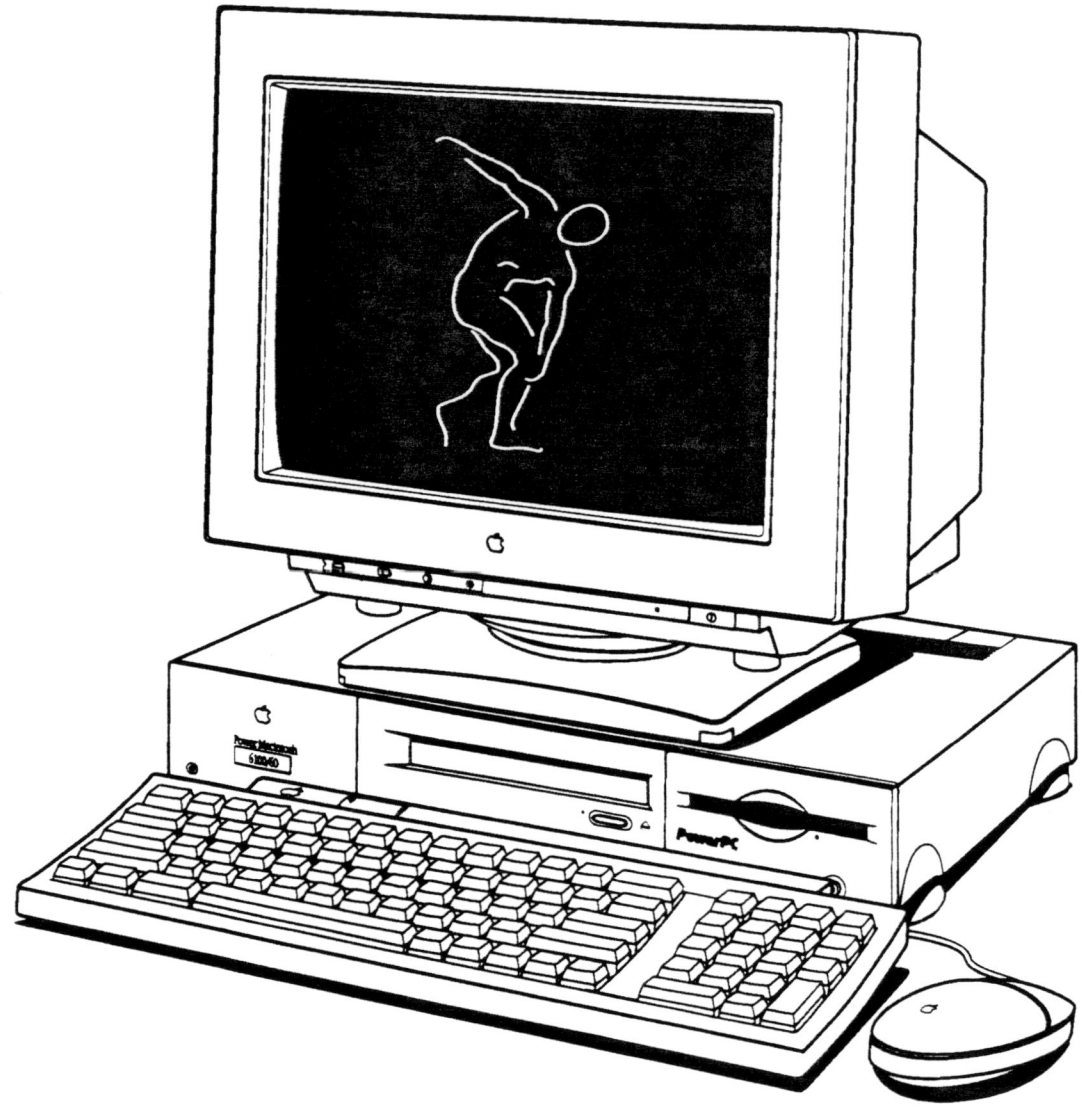

personal computer

pH A symbol used to express the acidity or alkalinity of a solution or material. On a scale of 0 to 14 the neutral point 7. Numbers less than 7 indicate an acid nature, while numbers greater than 7 indicate an alkaline nature. See *acid free paper*.

phonetics An alternate alphabet for pronunciation.

phosphor burn-in What occurs when the same image is left on the screen for extended periods of time, burning itself in so the image can be seen even when the monitor is turned off. See *screen saver*.

photocomposition The first phototypesetters were put into operation in the United States in 1953. They were invented by Louis Moyroud (France) and Rene Higonnet (France). See *phototypesetting*.

photocopy A copying or printing system that depends on an image formed from electrostatic charges. Powdered ink is attracted to the charged parts of a surface and then fused onto paper.

photostat A photocopy of the original artwork which gives an exact-size reproduction of the artwork.

phototypesetting A method of generating type that produces very high resolution characters and graphics.

pica Typographic unit of measurement equalling 12 points or 0.166 of an inch. Six picas equal approximately one inch; 72 points is equal to one inch.

pi characters Characters not usually found in a typical font, such as reference marks, mathematical symbols, special symbols, accents for foreign languages, bullets, stars, daggers, and fractions.

pi characters

pictograph A symbol representing an object.

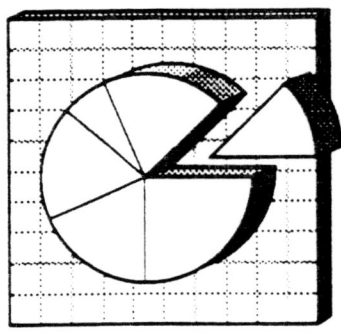

pie chart

pie chart Graphical representation of information; charting technique used to represent portions of a whole.

pin-feed Paper-feed system that relies on a pin-studded roller to draw paper, punched with matching sprocket holes, into a printer. See *tractor feed*.

piracy (1) Either theft, as in the appropriation of a computer design or a program, or unauthorized distribution and use of a computer program. (2) The copying and distribution of software to unauthorized users. (3) The printing and publishing of books by persons other than the copyright owner.

pitch Density of characters on a printed line, usually expressed in terms of characters per inch; for example, 10 pitch means that 10 characters are printed in every inch.

pixel Short for "picture element," a picture cell; a single dot on the computer display screen. The visual display screen is divided into rows and columns of tiny dots, squares, or cells, each of which is a pixel. Smallest unit on the display screen grid that can be stored, displayed, or addressed.

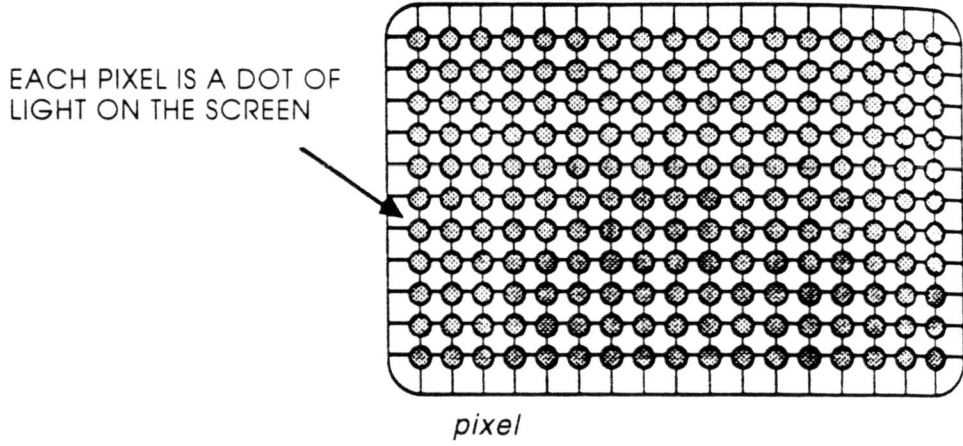

pixel

pixelated The equivalent of jaggies in low-resolution gray scale or color images. Instead of seeing "stair-steps," you can see each pixel and its gray level.

pixel depth The number of levels of gray or color possible in a bitmapped image. Literally, the number of bits it takes to describe each pixel.

pixel editing Changing the black, white, gray, or color orientation of a pixel.

pixel size The size of individual pixels on a computer graphic screen display. Pixel size is a function of monitor screen display size and display resolution.

plagiarism To copy, use or closely imitate another author's work, without compensation or permission, and represent it as your own. See *copyright infringement*, and *fair use*.

plain text Regular characters, as distinguished from italic, boldface, outline, shadow.

plastic binding A method of binding in which plastic teeth fit through notches in the pages. Also called *comb binding*.

plate Metal, paper, or plastic form etched with the elements of a page layout, for use on the printing press to transfer ink.

platen A backing, commonly cylindrical, against which printing mechanisms strike to produce an impression, such as the roller in a printer against which the keys strike.

plot To diagram, draw, or map with a plotter. To create an image by drawing a series of lines.

plotter An output device that draws images with ink pens. A plotter draws images as a series of point-to-point lines. Plotter types include: pen, drum, electrostatic, and flatbed.

PMS Acronym for Pantone Matching system, a standard system for the reproduction of colors with a system of premixed inks. Printed color swatches are assigned identification numbers. This system of color identification is widely used by the commercial printing and publishing industry. See *Pantone Matching System*.

point The basic typographic measuring unit (0.0138 inch) in which 12 points equal a pica and 72 points equal approximately one inch.

point and click To position the cursor over an object displayed on the screen (point) and press the mouse or pointing device to select it (click).

pointing device

pointing device An input device, such as a mouse, trackball, or graphics tablet that is used to move the cursor on the display screen.

point of purchase display A book display rack given to bookstores by publishers. Used to help promote a publisher's book.

point size The size of the type measured from the top of the ascender to the bottom of the descender; the size of a typefont.

Windsurfing   POINT SIZE

point size

point system There are three principal point systems in use differing basically in decimal detail. The American-British System, universally adopted by English speaking countries, has for its standard of measurement the 0.166 pica, and the 0.01383 point that is one-twelfth the pica. The Didot System, used in France, has the Cicero as its basic unit. The Mediaan System, used principally in Belgium, has a "corps" or point measurement of 0.01374.

point tool A tool used in layout and drawing programs to select objects or an entire block of text. It is usually represented by an on-screen arrow.

pop-up menu A menu that appears on-screen anywhere other than in the standard menu bar location.

port That portion of a computer through which a peripheral device may communicate. Plug-in/socket on the back of the computer for connecting cables for peripherals.

portable computer A self-contained computer that can be easily carried and moved. Compared to desktop models, it has limited expansion slots and disk capacity.

portfolio A collection of an illustrator's artwork, a photographer's photographs or a writer's publications.

portrait monitor A monitor with a screen shape higher than it is wide. A popular type monitor in desktop publishing systems.

portrait orientation An orientation in which the data has a height greater than its width. Contrast with *landscape orientation*. See *orientation*.

positive The opposite of a negative. An image that keeps the same gray-level orientation as the original. See *negative*.

portrait orientation

positive italic   The displayed attribute of leaning upward to the right. See *negative italic*.

poster   Another term for a leaflet.

posterization   A method of limiting the number of shades of gray in an image in order to create a special effect.

PostScript   A proprietary language developed by Adobe Corporation to tell a printer what to print on a particular page. PostScript's chief benefit is its device independence, that is to say that the same file can be printed to printers of varying resolutions.

PostScript laser printer   A laser printer that includes the processing circuitry needed to decode and interpret printing instructions phrased in PostScript — a page description language widely used in desktop publishing. The printer converts the PostScript instructions (sent by the computer) into the dots that make up the printer image.

PowerBook   A trademark for any of a group of Apple Macintosh laptop computers first released in 1992.

power down   (1) To turn off a computer or peripheral device. (2) Steps a computer may take to preserve the state of the processor and to prevent damage to it or to connected peripherals when the power fails or is shut off. Contrast with *power up*.

Power PC chip A computer chip, introduced in 1994, that was developed by an IBM-Apple Computer-Motorola alliance. As computers get smaller and smaller, the costs of developing the technology behind the trend are becoming too heavy for any corporation to bear alone. Thus, companies increasingly are combining forces to share the burden. See *Intel Corporation*.

power supply A device that provides power to electronic equipment such as computers and peripherals. Power supplies are rated by wattage, the higher the wattage, the stronger the power supply.

power surge A sudden, brief increase in the flow of current that can cause problems in the proper operation of computer equipment.

power up (1) To turn on a computer or peripheral device. (2) Steps taken by a computer processor when the power is turned on, or restored after a power failure. The processor and peripherals are initialized so that program execution may be started. Contrast with *power down*.

power user A computer user who has gone beyond the beginning and intermediate stages of computer use. Such a person uses the advanced features of application programs.

preface A section of frontmatter that, like a foreword or introduction, helps set the stage for the reader of a book. The preface often comments on the content of the book and how it should be used.

preferences Menu selections that let the computer user change measuring systems, grids, page sizes, and other characteristics of a design screen.

presentation graphics High quality professional looking business graphics. Used in proposals, business presentations, manuals and other business related documents. An easy-to-understand display of numerical information. Presentation graphics are visually appealing and easily understood by an audience.

Presentation Manager A graphical user interface (GUI) and application program interface (API) for OS/2. See *graphical user interface*.

pressboard A tough, dense, highly glazed paperboard, used where strength and stiffness are required of a relatively thin board. It is commonly used for the covers of notebooks.

press release An announcement sent by a book publisher to newspapers and magazines and other businesses to draw publicity for new books. Also called *news release*.

press run The quantity of sheets to be printed on a printing press. Also called print run.

preventive maintenance Maintenance done on a scheduled basis to prevent major problems. Involves cleaning and adjusting the equipment as well as testing the equipment, under both normal and marginal conditions.

primary letters Lower case letters without ascenders or descenders, such as a, c, e, m, etc.

printed resolution The quality of a computer graphic as output by a particular type of printer.

printer Output device that produces hardcopy output.

printer driver A device driver used to control a printer.

printer font A font available for printing. There are three types of printer fonts: built-in fonts, cartridge fonts, and downloadable fonts.

printer resolution The number of dots a laser printer can print on a linear inch. For example, most laser printers image at 300 dpi, while high-end imagesetters print at resolutions of 1270, 2540, and higher.

printing The process of reproducing textual, numerical or graphic matter by mechanical means.

printing origin Printing was already a widespread practice in China under the Tang Dynasty (618-907 A.D.): books on magic, scholastic manuals and so on were produced. The discovery in the Dunhuang caves of a copy of the *Diamond Sutra* printed in 868 A.D. gives us the name of the printer, Wang Zhe. Chinese printing prospered under the Sung Dynasty (960-1279), and in the year 1000, an important Buddhist Sutra was published. In 1041 Bi Sheng (China) made movable characters out of fired clay. The casting of metal characters was developed mostly in Korea around 1392. Around 1447 the printer Johann Gutenberg (1398-1468) developed, along with his associates, the technique of movable characters. In addition, he perfected the material necessary for the quality and conservation of characters: an alloy of lead, antimony and tin. In 1455, in Mainz, Germany, Guttenberg printed the *Biblia sacra latina*, known as the 42 line-per-page Bible. It was the first Latin edition of the Bible printed in movable characters. In 1477,

Helvetica
Helvetica Oblique
Helvetica Bold
Helvetica Bold Oblique
Times Roman
Times Italic
Times Bold
Times Bold Italic
Courier
Courier Oblique
Courier Bold
Courier Bold Oblique
Avant Garde Book
Avant Garde Book Oblique
Avant Garde Demi Bold
Avant Garde Demi Bold Oblique
Bookman Light
Bookman Light Italic
Bookman Demi Bold
Bookman Demi Bold Italic
Helvetica Narrow
Helvetica Narrow Oblique
Helvetica Narrow Bold
Helvetica Narrow Bold Oblique
New Century Schoolbook Roman
New Century Schoolbook Italic
New Century Schoolbook Bold
New Century Schoolbook Bold Italic
Palatino Roman
Palatino Italic
Palatino Bold
Palatino Bold Italic
Zapf Chancery Medium Italic
✻❋◻❈ ✢✣■✳☼✪▼▲

STANDARD FONTS THAT ARE RESIDENT ON MANY POSTSCRIPT LASER PRINTERS

printer font

William Caxton (1422-1491) set up the first printing press in Great Britain. The first printing press run by a steam machine was developed by F. Koenig (Germany) in 1812. Later, Koenig, in association with A. Bauer, constructed the first cylinder press, which was followed by many others. See *Fust, John, Gutenberg, Johann*, and *Schoeffer, Peter*.

print run   Number of copies to be printed.

process color   Printing that used only four standard colored inks to create the illusion of thousands of colors. See *full color process printing*.

processing   Computer manipulation of data in solving a problem.

processor   (1) The central processing unit of a computer. (2) In addition to the central processing unit, many sophisticated computer systems contain a dedicated processor for accelerated calculations.

process printing   The technique of breaking down color pictures into four separate component colors, making printing plates from halftone photographs of these components, and printing these plates in exact register to reproduce the picture, is called process printing.

professional books   Books written and published for professionals such as doctors, engineers, lawyers, etc.

program   Series of instructions that will cause a computer to process data. It may be in a high-level source form, which requires intermediate processing before the computer can execute it, or it may be in an object form directly executable by the computer.

prolog   An introduction to a book, usually placed in the front matter. This term is rarely used in books today. See *epilog*.

prompt   Any message output by a computer system that requires some response from the operator.

proof   A text copy of a printed sheet, which is used as a final check before a long reproduction run begins; an approval copy. A proof copy of a publication is used to identify errors.

proofreader   A person who checks type galleys and pages against the manuscript to make sure that it is correct.

proofreader's marks A standardized set of symbols used by copy editors and proofreaders to signify alterations and corrections in typeset copy.

⊙	Insert period
⌃	Insert comma
⊙	Insert colon
⌃	Insert semicolon
⌄	Apostrophe or 'single quote'
⌄⌄	Insert quotation marks
?/	Insert question mark
!/	Insert exclamation point
=/	Insert hyphen
⊥/M	Em dash
(/)	Insert parentheses
&	Insert ampersand (&)
wf	Wrong font (size or style of type)
lc	Lower case letter
≡	Capital letter
≡	SET IN capitals
Caps/lc	Lower Case with Initial Capitals
Caps/sc	SMALL CAPITALS WITH INITIAL CAPS
rom	Set in roman type
ital	Set in italic type
u/s	Set underscore
LF	Set in lightface type
¶	Begin new paragraph
No ¶	No paragraph. Run in or run on
#	Insert space (or more space)
⏋	Set further to right
⌐	Set further to left
⏋⌐	Put in center of line or page
[{	Flush left Flush right }⏋
//	Straighten line (horizontally)
‖	Align type (vertically) ⌐
trs	Transpose space

proofreader's marks

proofreading The process of reading a proof to detect mistakes in spelling, punctuation, style, font, size, etc. and marking corrections on the proof.

proportional font A font with varying size widths for letters. The letter I takes less width than the letter W. See *monofont*.

proportional sizing A proportion is the relation, or ratio, of one part to another and of each part to the whole with regard to size, height, width, length, or depth. Most graphics programs allow you to resize and reshape graphic objects on the display screen. Proportional sizing should be used whenever you wish a scaled image to keep proper dimensions, otherwise the scaled image will be distorted.

proportional spacing If the horizontal space allotted to a printed character is proportional to the width of that character, the spacing is said to be proportional. Since this book is typeset in proportional spacing, the "w" in the word "write" consumes more space than the "i." Standard typewriter style, in contrast, allots equal space to all characters.

```
PROPORTIONAL SPACING

    Now is the

FIXED SPACING (MONOSPACING)

   N ow  is  the
```

proportional spacing

PS/2 See *IBM Personal System/2*.

publication A document created with a desktop publishing software, books, brochures, newsletters, magazines and maps are all publications.

public domain publications Publications which were either never copyrighted or whose copyright term has expired, and thus available for use by the public.

public domain software Software not protected by copyright laws and therefore free for all to reproduce and trade without fear of legal prosecution. Any computer program donated to the public by its creator. Public domain software may be duplicated by others at will.

publish To produce and sell or otherwise make publications available to an audience.

publisher (1) An organization or person (self-publisher) that created, designs, produces and distributes publications. (2) Chief executive officer or owner of a publishing company.

Publishers Marketing Association (PMA) PMA is a nonprofit association of book, audio, and video publishers. It is a cooperative marketing organization that provides marketing information and combined advertising programs for a variety of small to medium-sized publishers nationally.

publishing book Genuine publishing houses already existed in ancient Greek and Roman times. Athens and Rome boasted printed works of which several hundred copies were published. It was, of course, only with the invention of the industrial print shop that publishing really began to flourish, and the bookshop came soon after. The latter was born in London with the bookstore of Wynkyn de Worde, successor to William Caxton, and publisher of the first book to be produced in English in Great Britain, in 1495. But it was not until the late 16th century that bookshops began to specialize in selling books from one field or another, and it was only then that publishers charged them with the task of distributing their products.

publishing cycle The movement of a document from creation to final printing.

puck Hand-held, manually controlled, graphics input device used to pinpoint coordinates on a digitizing tablet. Has a transparent window containing cross hairs and allows coordinate data to be digitized into the system from a drawing placed on the digitizing tablet surface.

pull-down menu A second-level menu, or list of commands, that appears from the top of the screen when a command needs to be given and then disappears when the selection has been made. A pull-down menu is usually used as an extension to a menu bar. To select an option on a pull-down menu, one presses and holds down the mouse button while dragging the mouse pointer down the menu until the wanted option is highlighted.

pull quote A typographic embellishment used in newsletters and magazines in which an excerpt from the surrounding text is enlarged and offset for emphasis.

quad A unit of space. To quad is to align a block of type left, right, or center.

Quark XPress A page layout program for the Apple Macintosh computer from Quark, Inc. It is noted for its precise typographic control and sophisticated graphics capabilities. Quark XPress allows unlimited document length and includes many word processing features.

QuickDraw A graphics language system built into the ROM of the Apple Macintosh computer. Application programs call on QuickDraw for on-screen displays. QuickDraw consists of a series of primitive shapes, lines, and fill patterns which can be mathematically modified. When printing to PostScript printers, QuickDraw must be translated during the printing process by a program called a PostScript interpreter.

quit (1) To exit the current application program. (2) An action that tells a system to return to a previous state or stop a process.

quotes Opening and closing punctuation marks to indicate verbal statements or to define or emphasize certain words.

QWERTY keyboard Keyboard arrangement that is standard on most keyboards found on typewriters, word processors, and computers. Developed more than a century ago to slow down swift typists and prevent jamming of the old mechanical typewriters. The design is called QWERTY after the first six letters on the top alphabetic line of the keyboard. Now that electronics can accommodate high-speed typing, QWERTY is no longer efficient. Many businesses are replacing QWERTY keyboards with the more efficient *Dvorak keyboard*. Some computer companies now offer keyboards with a switch that will change form one keyboard to the other. See *Dvorak keyboard* and *Maltron keyboard*.

R

radial gradient A gradual fade in all directions from a specific central point.

ragged Unjustified. The setting of text type with an irregular appearance on either one or both margins. In the ragged setting, interword spaces are not varied for justification. Ragged setting is the opposite of flush setting in which even margins are achieved on both sides of the text. Compare with *justified*.

ragged bottom Letting the last line fluctuate in position, from page to page.

ragged left alignment Refers to text printed with a straight right margin and an uneven left margin. Also called *flush right*.

ragged right alignment Text printed with a straight left margin and an uneven right margin Also called *flush left*.

ragging The setting of irregular shaped blocks of type by varying the left and right margins.

American printer, publisher, author,
inventor, scientist and diplomat.
Benjamin Franklin is best remembered
for his role in separating the
American colonies from Great Britain
and in helping to frame
the Declaration of Independence.
raised initial

raised initial A very large, graphic character on the baseline of a first line of text. Used at the start of a book chapter, section or occasional paragraph.

RAM Acronym for Random Access Memory, a memory into which the user can enter information and instructions (write) and from which the user can call up data (read). Working memory of the computer, into which applications programs can be loaded form outside and then executed.

raster graphics Manner of storing and displaying data as horizontal rows of uniform grid or picture cells (pixels). Raster scan devices recreate or refresh a display screen thirty to sixty times a second to provide clear images for viewing. Raster display devices are generally faster and less expensive than vector tubes.

rasterization The process of converting outlines into bitmaps. The outlines are scaled to the desired size and filled by turning on pixels inside the outline.

ratio The size relationship between height and width.

raw copy A manuscript or some other form of copy to be set in type.

ray tracing In computer graphics, a method of adding a degree of realism to an image through the use of reflections, refractions, and shadows. A sophisticated and complex approach to producing high-quality computer graphics. Ray tracing is a very process-intensive operation.

RC (Resin-Coated) paper Photographic paper used for typesetting and imagesetting. Like film, it must be developed. It can then be pasted up to a mechanical and photographed using a graphic arts camera.

read To get information from any input or file storage media, such as reading a floppy diskette by sensing the patterns of magnetism. Contrast with *write*.

readability The ease with which information or type can be read. Factors affecting readability include type size and spacing.

read-in A design for cutlines in which the display type is part of a sentence that is continued in body size type.

read-only memory (ROM) Special type of computer memory, permanently programmed with one group of frequently used instructions. Does not lose its program when the computer's power is turned off, but the program cannot be changed by the user.

readouts (1) A section of text that is set apart from the main copy and is used as a graphic element. It emphasizes an important quote or statement from within the main body of an article and is typeset in a display typeface. (2) A small headline between the main headline and the story.

read-through A style for outlines in which the opening phrase is set in boldface or capital letters or both.

ream Five hundred sheets of paper; common package size for 8.5- by 11-inch paper.

reboot To stop and boot the operating system again. Usually occurs by human intervention as the result of a problem. Similar to "reset" on a home appliance. To restart.

record Collection of related items of data treated as a unit. Description of an item in a database. Each item is represented by a record that consists of one or more fields. Everyday examples of a record include an entry in a dictionary or a listing in a phone book.

recover Commonly used to describe the process of restoring lost or damaged files.

recto Latin for the right-hand page, opposite of verso.

recto/verso A right-hand and left-hand format for documents intended to be viewed as left-reading and right-reading. Page numbering and titles change from left to right as well as gutters and outer margins.

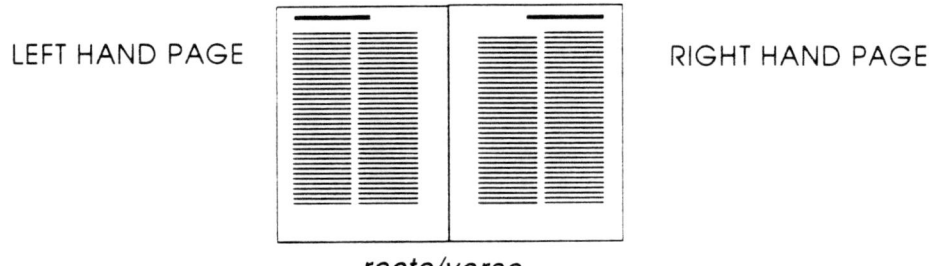

recto/verso

recycled paper New paper made entirely or in part from old paper.

red-pencil To correct or revise typeset copy.

reduce To make an image or text smaller.

reduced instruction set computer (RISC) A microprocessor that has only a relatively small set of instructions. RISC design is based on the premise that most of the instructions a computer decodes and executes are simple, thus RISC architecture limits the number of instructions that are built into the microprocessor but optimizes each so it can be carried out very rapidly.

reference book A book containing reference information. For example, a dictionary, an encyclopedia, an almanac or a thesaurus.

reference marks Symbols used instead of superior figures to mark footnotes.

reference section A section of a book layout containing the appendix, bibliography, glossary of terms, etc.

reflective art Any image that is viewed by reflected light such as a drawing or photograph on paper, as opposed to transparencies which are illuminated by light shining through. Reflective art includes: black-and-white photos, color prints, line art, etc.

reformat To change the representation of data from one format to another.

refreshing Process of constantly reactivating or restoring information that decays or fades away when left idle. Phosphor on a CRT screen needs to be constantly reactivated by an electron beam to remain illuminated. Typically, the image must be regenerated at a rate of 30 to 60 hertz to avoid flicker. Likewise, cells in dynamic memory elements must be repeatedly accessed to avoid losing their contents.

register The precise alignment of the color plates in a multicolor printing.

register marks Marks used to permit exact alignment of pages. Usually printed just outside the live area and then trimmed off. The standard register mark is a small circle with a cross inside.

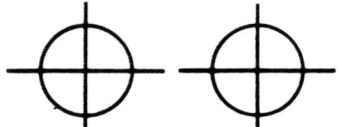

register marks

registration Seamless alignment of multistage printing such as two or more colors. Achieved by aligning master registration marks on each piece of camera-ready work. See r*egister marks*.

release number The number that identifies a specific version of a program. A program labeled 3.5, for example is the sixth release of Version 3 of the program (the first was Version 3.0).

remainders Unsold copies of books marked down below the original retail price and sold for a fraction of their cover price.

removable storage Diskettes, hard disk cartridges, or optical disk cartridges that can be removed from the device that reads data from them or writes data to them.

rename To change the file name on disk.

rendering The actual placement of rasterized pixels on the monitor's display. Refers both to graphic objects and type, particularly for fonts using hints. Also called *rasterization*.

repagination Where a multipaged document is renumbered and reformatted to provide uniform page length.

repeat key Keyboard key that can be held down so it repeatedly makes contact without need for additional pressing.

repertoire The set of available characters in a font, or commands in a program, or some other group of functions.

replace Command that enables a user to search for a word and replace it with another one.

report Usually associated with output data; involves the grouping of related facts so as to be easily understood by the reader. Common means of presenting information to users. Most reports are on-screen display or printed listings showing selected information extracted from a database.

reprint rights The rights to republish a book.

reproduce To make a copy from an original.

reproduction copy Alternate term for *camera ready copy*.

reprographics A branch of graphic arts that is concerned with the reproduction of images and especially making photocopies from an original document. See *xerography*.

reseller Anyone who sells computer products.

reset button A button on many computers used to reboot the computer without turning off the power.

resident font A font that resides permanently in the read-only memory (ROM) of a printer. Compare with soft font.

resident program Program that occupies a dedicated area of a computer's main memory (ROM or RAM) during the operating session.

resize To alter the height, the width, or the overall size of an existing art image.

resolution The resolution of a printer or display screen is a measure of the sharpness of the images it can produce.

resolution

resource Any component of a computer configuration. Memory, printers, visual displays, disk storage units, software, materials, and operating personnel are all considered resources.

response Information entered at a prompt.

resume A printed summary of educational background and work experience.

retrieving Process of making stored information available when needed.

Return See *Enter key*.

returns Books returned to the publishers by bookstores and wholesalers.

reverse White letters on a black background; light colored letters on a dark colored background; or dark colors on a bright background.

reverse kicker A short one-line head, which is twice as large as the main head, that is placed below and indented to the right.

reverse print Having white type or graphics on a black background (or some variation on that theme) instead of the usual black type or graphics on a white background.

review copy A free copy of a book sent by the publisher to a potential reviewer.

rhythm In the context of graphic communications design, rhythm refers to eye movement. Elements can be designed and placed to direct the reader's eye to the desired location on the page, to the most important part of the message. The shape, size and positioning of graphic and text elements can direct the reader's eye vertically, horizontally, or at an angle.

right opener The initial page of a chapter or article beginning on a recto (right-facing) page.

right justification A method of aligning text so that each line of text is flush against the right margin, leaving a ragged or uneven left margin.

ring network One of the three principal topologies for a local area network, in which each computer is connected to other computers, forming a continuous loop or circle. See b*us network, network,* and *star network.*

RIP An acronym for Raster Image Processor, converts fonts and graphics into raster images, which are used by the printer to draw onto the page.

RISC Short for Reduced Instruction Set Computer, a computer system designed to minimize the number of different underlying operations that the microprocessor does in hardware in order to optimize the execution speed. Such systems depend on the software for functions that formerly were handled by the microprocessor.

river A snake-like area of white space created when several consecutive lines contains words that break in the same position.

ROM Acronym for Read-Only Memory. Generally, a solid state storage chip programmed at the time of its manufacture and that cannot be reprogrammed by the computer user. Also called firmware, since this implies software that is permanent or firmly in place on a chip.

roman A font that is upright, thick-and-thin weighted, and usually serifed type. The classical Roman letter style began in A.D. 114 with letters chiseled in the stone of the Trajan Columns in Rome, Italy. Roman fonts have no style applied to it (i.e., Italic, Bold, Bold Italic).

Roman numerals Roman letters in current use as numerals until the tenth century AD I, II, III, IV, V, VI, etc. In traditional book design, lowercase Roman numerals (i, ii, iii, iv, v, vi, vii, etc.) are used to identify the pages in the frontmatter of books.

rotated text Text that has been turned about one or more axes. Rotated text can be used effectively in a variety of situations.

rough layout Loosely drawn ideas by a designer. Usually several rough layouts are sketched out before an idea is agreed upon and a comprehensive is developed from them.

royalty Payments made to an author by a publisher for books which have been sold, based on a percentage of the price of the book.

rule A typographic element in the form of a line. Used for boxes, borders, or as a line to write on in a form.

run Single or continuous execution of a program by a computer on a given set of data. See *execute*.

runaround Type set to fit around an illustration, a box, an irregular shape, or any other graphic element.

runaround

running Continuing; for instance running headers and footers appear on every page.

running feet A book title or chapter name repeated on the bottom of each page.

running head A book title or chapter head repeated at the top of every page in a book. It is sometimes an abbreviated form of the full title. See *header*.

run on (1) Instruction for text to continue without a new paragraph. A run-on chapter is one which does not begin on a new page. (2) Merging two paragraphs.

saddle stitch A means of binding by stapling sheets together where they fold at the spine.

sales representative A salesperson who represents a publisher's books to book retailers, book wholesalers, etc., in exchange for a commission.

sans serif Letters of typefaces without serifs — the ornate, widened bases and tops seen on some characters of some type fonts. As a matter of fact, sans means "without" in French. Sans serif fonts have very clean lines and are typically considered friendly, casual and familiar.

SERIF **BOX** **BOX** SANS SERIF
sans serif

save To store information somewhere other than in the computer's internal memory, such as on disk, so it can be used again.

sc Abbreviation for small capitals.

scalable A graphic image, usually outline or vector, capable of being scaled down or up to different sizes.

scalable font Characters which can be scaled to any size via a page description language. By contrast, bitmap fonts must be loaded for every size, using up storage space. Scalable fonts provide more flexibility than bit-mapped fonts by eliminating the need to store a variety of different font sizes in the computer's memory.

scaling Changing the size of an image while maintaining its original proportions. Scaling by a factor of three multiplies all dimensions of an image by 3.

scanned image A bit-mapped, or TIFF, image generated by an optical scanner. Many layout programs can scale or crop scanned images before placing them into a page.

scanner An optical reading device that can recognize text, drawings and photographs and convert them into electronic representation of the images. Scanners can be differentiated by whether they process color or are limited to shades of gray. Scanner resolution is determined by the amount of information available from the scanning sensor for a given area. Common resolutions in desktop scanners are 200-600 dots per inch. More powerful systems can scan up to 8000 lines per inch or more.

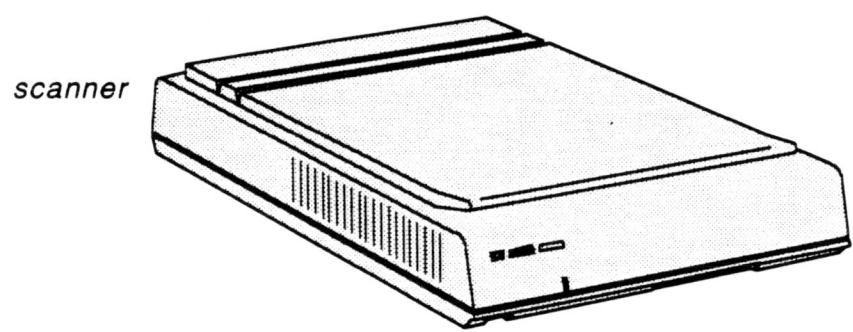

scanner

scattergram A graph using a pattern of dots to show the relationship between two sets of data.

Schoeffer, Peter One of the three persons commonly regarded as the inventors of printing. He was in the employment of Johann Gutenberg in Mentz, Germany for some time, and after John Fust took possession of the printing office he continued working there. See *Gutenberg, Johann* and *John Fust*.

score To compress paper along a straight line so it folds more easily and accurately.

scrap To discard.

scrapbook A storage location for frequently used text and pictures. The stored images can be inserted into new documents as required.

screamer Another term for a large *banner* head.

screen capture (1) The transfer of the image on the current display screen into a graphics file. (2) A printout of the current screen display.

screen cursor An indicating symbol generated by the display hardware and moved by the user around the screen area. Its position on the screen can be made to correspond to the position of a hand-held input device, such as a mouse moved across a mouse pad.

screen dump Process of transferring the information currently appearing on a display screen to a printer or saved as a file on disk; to a "snapshot" of the screen.

screen flicker The appearance of a flicker or other distortion on a computer display screen.

screen fonts The bitmapped representations of a printer font that is used to display the font on the screen. A screen font is designed to mimic the appearance of printer fonts when displayed on medium-resolution monitors.

screen memory A portion of RAM that stores data needed to display whatever is output to the display screen.

screen resolution A measure of the crispness of images and characters on a screen, usually specified in terms of the number of pixels in a row or column.

screen saver A program that produces moving patterns on the screen after a specified number of minutes without keyboard or mouse activity. Pressing a key on the keyboard or moving the mouse restores the screen. Screen savers are used to prolong the life of a monitor; they prevent one image from being burned into the screen phosphors. See also *phosphor burn-in*.

script Decorative typeface resembling handwriting. Since script is difficult to read, its use should be limited to a few lines at a time. Early script typefaces were developed in the sixteenth century, and, were based upon formal cursive handwriting.

Script   Script

script

scrolling The vertical or horizontal movement of information (text or graphics) on a display screen in order to bring different parts of the page into view.

SCSI Acronym for Small Computer Systems Interface. The SCSI is a general purpose parallel interface designed for connecting one or more computers and one or more peripherals — a total of 8 devices may be connected to one bus.

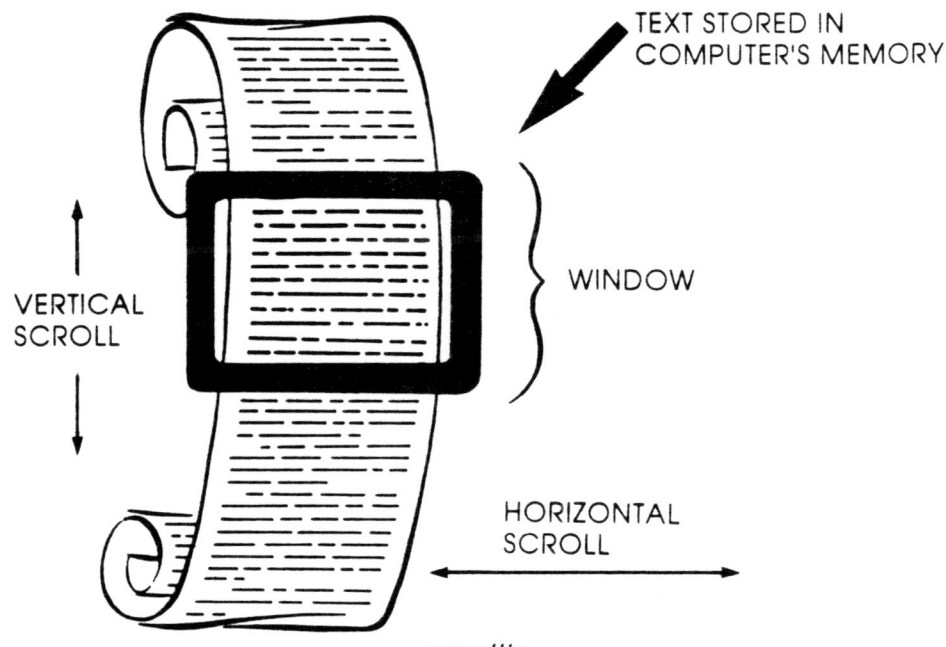
scrolling

search and replace Software feature that finds a designated character sequence and replaces it with a new one. Important in word processing applications.

secondary illustration Any illustration other than the main illustration.

secondary storage device A machine, such as a disk unit, mass storage device, tape unit, capable of providing storage to supplement primary memory.

sector The smallest unit of storage on a disk. Disks are divided into sectors and tracks. The address where data is stored is made up of the sector and track number.

select To designate where the next action will take place, often done by using a keyboard, mouse or trackball.

self-publish To publish one's own work.

self-publisher A writer who is his or her own publisher.

semiconductor A material that can act either as a conductor or non-conductor of electricity depending on the level of current. Silicon is a semiconductor.

serif An ending stroke on the arms, tails and stems of characters in certain typeface designs. Serif type styles are typically considered businesslike, formal, and authoritative.

SERIF TYPEFACE  SANS SERIF TYPEFACE

serif

service bureau An organization that provides data processing services, business software development or pre-press services to its customers.

set close Instruction to set type with the minimum of space between the individual characters and words.

set solid Text set with zero leading. For example, 11 point type on 11 point leading.

setup Alternate term for *makeready*.

set-width The width of a letter and its surrounding space, the space needed to set a line of text in a specific typeface.

shade A degree of tint or pattern used to fill an area.

shaded type A typeface designed with a drop shadow or a drop outline to give a three dimensional appearance.

ABCDEFGHIJKLMNOPQR

shaded type

shadow box A box with a screen tint along two sides to create the illusion of a shadow.

shadow face A typeface ornamented with additions outside of the strokes of the character. A character looks as if the letter were three dimensional, with a light on the side, casting a shadow.

shadow face

shareware Software that is passed around. The authors let you copy and share their programs freely, but retain the copyrights. Shareware provides income to its author in the form of "contributions," much like public TV. Payment is strictly voluntary. Even though shareware is given away free, the maker hopes that satisfied users will voluntarily pay for it.

sharpness (1) Clarity and quality of an image produced on a visual display device, digital plotter, printer, film recorder, and other devices. See *resolution*. (2) The degree of clarity of a photographic image.

sheet feeder Device that attaches to the printer, designed to automatically insert and line up single sheets of paper or envelopes in much the same way as an operator would perform the task. Usually sits above the printer platen and is operated either mechanically or electrically by the printer.

Shift key The keyboard key you press to enter uppercase letters or punctuation marks.

shilling The oblique line used to separate one element from another in type. Also called slash, virgule, fraction bar and solidus.

shilling fraction A fraction created by using standard sized numerals for the numerator and denominator, and separating them by a shilling mark, e.g., 3/4.

short run Relatively small quantity to print in relation to the size and speed of the printing machine used.

shotgun head A single headline over two decks, each with its own story below.

show through Printing on one side of a sheet that is visible from the other side due to insufficient opacity of the paper.

shrink wrap A clear plastic film covering heat shrunk to fit tightly over a book or other product. One method of protecting the covers of books when they are shipped.

shrink-wrapped software A ready-to-use software product that is packaged and ready for sale.

side A printing surface of a piece of paper.

sidebar In a book, magazine or newsletter, a separate but related article in conjunction with a larger story, often offset by a screen or box rule; a short article that is used to give particular information concerning a related point in the main body of the article.

sidebar

side bearing The space between the origin of a character and its leftmost point (left side bearing), or the space between the rightmost point and width line (right side bearing).

sideless box A decorative rule or border at the top and bottom of a block of type.

side staple A method of binding a publication by stapling through the side of the publication on the binding edge.

signature An eight-, sixteen-, or thirty-two page group of pages which results from a printing press sheet being folded and cut. Most books are made up of several signatures of pages.

silhouette The outline of an object filled in with black or another solid color.

silhouette

single sided publication A publication with pages reproduced on one side only of each sheet of paper.

single user One person at one time using a computer.

sinkage The deep gap that may appear between the top of a text area and the top of the first element on a page — usually a chapter title or section title.

size range The span of point sizes a desktop publishing system can set.

skew (1) To slant an element horizontally, vertically or both. (2) Misalignment of alphanumeric characters.

skyline A headline.

slab serif A type of font in which characters have rectangular serifs.

slug line A significant word or phrase that is used to identify a story through its processing.

slant A mark used between parts of a fraction, for example 3/4.

slash The oblique line used to separate one element from another in type.

slipcase A protective open-ended box in which a book or set of books are placed and sold as a unit.

slip-sheet To insert blank sheets between printed sheets or sets of printed sheets. Also called interleave.

small caps Capital letters that are the same (or nearly the same) height as the typeface's x-height.

smoothing A technique used for eliminating jaggies, the jagged distortions that appear on curves.

Smyth sewing The method of book binding in which the pages are sewn together with thread and then glued onto the cover.

soft cover A heavy paper cover for a booklet, paperback book, report or other publication.

soften An electronic effect that blurs the contrast around the edges of an image.

soft font A font that is downloaded from a computer to a printer from files stored on a disk. Compare with *font cartridge*.

soft hyphen Conditional (nonrequired) hyphen printed only to break a word between syllables at the end of a line. Contrast with *hard hyphen*. Same as *discretionary hyphen*.

soft page break A page break inserted by the program.

soft return Combination line feed/carriage return command, entered by a program containing the word wrap feature to begin a new line within a paragraph. Unlike a hard return, it is conditional — the computer executes the command only when the current word doesn't fit in the line in progress.

software The generic term for any computer program or programs; instructions that cause the hardware to do work. Contrast with the "iron" or hardware of a computer system.

software developer A person or firm that develops and markets software for profit.

software package A prewritten program that can be purchased for use with a specific computer to perform a specific task. Usually includes the programs, stored on a storage media (floppy disk, CD-ROM and so on), and an operating manual.

software piracy The illegal copying and distribution of copyrighted software.

software upgrade A new, enhanced version of a developer's software. It usually contains features and functions not found in the earlier release.

solid leading No additional white space is added/between lines of type; type set without additional line spacing.

solidus A mark used between parts of a fraction (e.g., 5/8).

spacing The amount of unused space that exists between words, letters, and lines in text.

special effects A general term for reproduction of photographs using techniques such as posterization, stipple, or mezzotint.

spec sheet A list of printing specifications from which a printing business makes an estimate of price for a job.

spelling checker Computer program, usually associated with word processing, that compares typed words against a word list and informs the user of possible spelling mistakes. A sophisticated spelling checker can have a base dictionary of well over 100,000 words and can provide the user with the ability to create special-purpose dictionaries of words not included in the base dictionary.

spike A very short transient electrical signal, often of very high amplitude. See *power surge, surge* and *surge protector*.

spillover Text that exceeds the boundaries of a text block.

spine (1) The bound edge of a book; the part of a book binding visible when the book is shelved. (2) The main curved arc section of the letter S.

splice To lengths of paper joined together.

spline A mathematically defined curve that smoothly links a series of dots.

split screen Display screen that can be partitioned into two or more areas (windows) so different screen formats can be shown on the screen at the same time. It implies that one set of data can be manipulated independently of the other.

spot color A single color applied during printing to specified areas of the artwork.

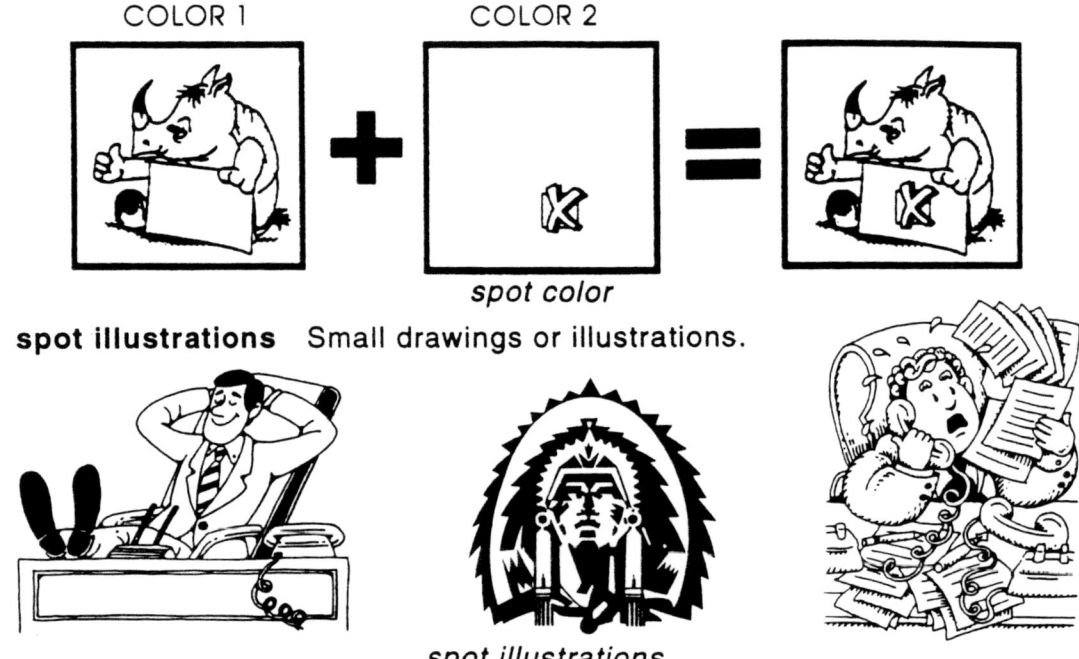

spot color

spot illustrations Small drawings or illustrations.

spot illustrations

spread Two pages (left- and right-hand) that appear side by side in a page layout. The two pages are designed to go together.

spreadsheet A software program that simulates a paper spreadsheet or worksheet, in which columns of numbers are summed for budgets and plans. A spreadsheet appears on screen as a matrix of rows and columns in which each intersection is defined as a cell.

spur A finishing stroke like the ones on certain uppercase "G"s.

square serif Typefaces that have squared-off serifs on the characters' end strokes. Also called "Egyptian."

SRAM An acronym for Static Random Access Memory. Unlike a DRAM, a SRAM does not need constant reactivating to save the information in its millions of cells. The Japanese companies Sony, HItachi and Toshiba are producing 4-bit SRAMS. See *DRAM*.

S.S. Abbreviation for Same Size.

stack Single letters or lines of type one on the other.

stagger Letters set at alternating slants.

stamp To imprint by using a die.

standalone computer (1) Self-contained computer system that can work independently, not connected to or under the control of another computer system. A standalone system contains all the hardware and software a user requires. (2) Not connected to a network, or operating as if not connected to a network.

stand-off The distance between runaround text and the graphic it is running around.

standing elements The elements that appear in every issue of a publication.

star network One of the three principal topologies for a local area network, in which all computers and devices, known as nodes, are connected to one central computer, known as the hub. All communication between nodes is routed by the hub. See *bus network, network*, and *ring network*.

startup disk Diskette that contains the information to start the computer system.

stat Short for photostat, an inexpensive photographic print of line copy or halftone.

status line A line of an application program's display screen that describes the state of the program.

stem The upright element of a letter or character, as in the center stroke of the letter T. On a letter formed by strokes of varying thickness, the stem refers to the thick strokes.

stepped heads A design in which the first line of a headline is set flush left; the last flush right and middle line, if used, is centered.

step up/step down Words typeset at increasing or decreasing fixed percentages to create a three dimensional effect.

stet A proofreading term meaning to disregard correction mark. Latin word meaning "let it stand" or "ignore requested correction."

stickup initial A decorative initial letter at the beginning of a paragraph that rises above the top of the first line.

sticky space A character that tells the program to keep two words together.

stipple Pattern of dots of various sizes. An illustration might be stippled as a special effect.

stock Another name for paper.

stock photography Photography that is supplied by stock photo collections as opposed to photography that is commissioned.

stock photography

storage Descriptive of a device or medium that can accept data, hold it, and deliver it on demand at a later time. The term is preferred over memory.

story A chain of linked text that occupies one or more columns or pages.

straddle To cross over. Some programs can let a title spread across (or straddle) three columns; others limit a title to one column.

straight copy Copy that is all text with no illustrations.

streaming cartridge A high-speed tape backup system, often used to make a complete backup of an entire hard disk.

street price The current price of a computer product at a computer store, mail order business, or other retail business. The street price of a product is often considerably lower than the retail price of a product. It is an average price charged by dealers around the country.

stress The vertical, horizontal, or diagonal emphasis on the stroke of a letter; variations between thick and thin strokes of a type character.

strikethrough A technique that prints a hyphen over each character to indicate a deletion while the text remains readable.

stripping Assembling and positioning elements within negatives from which printing plates will be made.

stroke (1) The major lines that make up a character. (2) One line segment in a vector graphic image.

stroke weight The level of thickness in the lines of a font. Also called *line weight*.

style A visual variation of a basic typeface used to create emphasis. Type style is important since it can attract (or repel) the reader's eye. The four basic computer styles are Plain, *Italic*, **Bold**, and ***Bold Italic***.

style sheet A file that contains formatting instructions but not text. Style sheets contain such information as margin sizes, column widths, paragraph indention, spacing, fonts, size, and style. Applying a stylesheet to text automatically formats the text according to the stylesheet's specifications.

stylus In computer graphics, a pointer that you operate by placing it in a display space or a graphics tablet. To draw a point, the user touches the stylus (also called a pen) tip to the surface of the graphics tablet. The stylus and graphics tablet are preferred drawing devices for artists.

subhead Usually located beneath the headline as secondary information or as summarizing phrases between sections of text.

subscript Type that is generally smaller than regular text placed at or below the baseline as in a footnote reference.

subsidiary rights Rights, other than book publishing rights included in a book publishing contract, such as foreign rights, book club rights, mass paperback rights, movie rights, etc.

subsidy publisher A company that charges writers to publish their book, then usually retains ownership of the books and does little, if any, promotion. They are the "bad guys" of book publishing. Hundreds of book publishing horror stories have been documented about subsidy publishers. Also called *vanity publisher*.

superscript Type of a smaller size than text placed at or near the cap height for special references.

SUPERSCRIPT   SUBSCRIPT

10^{21} H_2O

superscript

Super VGA High-resolution video display standard for IBM Personal Computers and compatibles.

support The assistance provided by a hardware or software vendor in installing, maintaining and learning their product.

surge A sudden and often destructive increase in line voltage. See *spike*..

surge protector Device that protects electrical equipment from being damaged by short surges of high voltage by filtering them out. A computer or other device is plugged into the surge protector, which itself is plugged into a standard electrical outlet. Also called surge suppressor.

surprint Printing text or graphics over a lighter halftone, a graphic, or a screen tint.

swash capitals

swash capitals Uppercase letters that have fancy flourishes, extended serifs, or other decorative features added to them. Originally designed to go with Italic typefaces. Intended for use at the beginning or end of a single word.

symmetrical design A basic design structure where all elements are centered on a page. Symmetry is order, balance — all elements in harmony. Asymmetry is the opposite, with no predictable pattern.

system

system A group of related components that interact to perform a task. A computer system is made up of the CPU, memory, operating system, software, and peripheral devices.

system disk The disk that contains the operating system and other systems programs that are necessary to start the computer.

system prompt In an operating system such as DOS, the prompt that indicates the operating system's availability for entering commands.

system software Programs that run the computer system and aid the user in doing his/her task.

System 7 Operating system for the Apple Macintosh computer. System 7 expands the Macintosh capabilities including an upgraded finder, file sharing capability, truetype fonts, inter-application communications and virtual memory.

tab Carriage control that specifies output columns.

table A typeset chart, often divided by horizontal and vertical rules.

table of contents A table in the frontmatter section of a book showing the location of chapters and main topics.

table of illustrations A table in the frontmatter section of a book showing a list of all illustrations and page numbers.

tabloid A newspaper about half the size of a regular newspaper.

tabular Tabular composition in essentially vertical alignment within multiple columns.

tag A collection of specifications applied to a paragraph that determines its font, alignment, spacing, ruling lines, and other features.

tagged image file format (TIFF) A common file format used to store bit-mapped graphic images. TIFF simulates gray-scale shading.

tagline A comment that explains a logo, e.g., the subtitle of a newsletter.

tail A character's downward projection such as on the letters "Q,", "R," or "K."

tape Strip of material that may be coated with a magnetically sensitive substance and used for data input, storage, or output. Data are usually stored serially in several channels across the tape, transversely to the reading or writing motion.

tape backup A device that uses magnetic tape to back up files.

TARGA A high resolution color raster imagefile format used primarily by paint programs.

target (1) The desired destination. (2) The place to which information is supposed to be copied. (3) Something that is being searched for.

target printer The printer selected for printing the final version of a publication or document.

teacher's manual A guide that supplements a specific textbook. The guide is used by teachers to aid them in using the textbook in the classroom.

tear-off menu A screen menu that can be moved off its primary position, relocated to any part of the display screen and kept active.

technical support Technical advise provided to registered users of a hardware device or program. Many computer companies offer technical support for the products they manufacture.

telecommunications Transfer of data from one place to another over long distances, using telephone lines, microwaves and/or satellites.

template (1) Plastic sheet placed over keyboard keys to help the user remember tasks performed by each key. (2) In page layout and word processing programs, templates are predesigned page formats. You use the template by loading the file, adding the text and/or graphic images, and printing; a master publication design format. (3) A dummy publication that acts as a model, providing the structure and general layout for another similar publication.

terabyte One trillion or 1,099,511,627,776 bytes or characters. It is abbreviated TB.

terminal An input/output device for a computer that usually has a keyboard for input and a video screen for output.

terminals Not serifs but ends of certain letter shapes such as the letters "f," "j," "y," "r," and "a."

text blocks In a desktop publishing program, an area in which typing can be done.

text composition Evenly spaced lines, usually set in the same type size and style.

text editing General term that covers any additions, changes, or deletions made to electronically stored material.

text editor Computer program used to manipulate text; for example, to erase, insert, change, and move words or groups of words. The manipulated text may be another computer program.

text file File containing information expressed in text form. Same as *data file*.

text type Words, sentences, paragraphs, and numbers that express the information to be conveyed. Text is the major portion of most publications. Also called *body type*.

text wrap A feature supported by some word processing and desktop publishing programs that allows you to contour type around a graphic.

thermal wax-transfer printer A nonimpact printer that uses heat to melt colored wax onto paper to create an image. It uses pins to apply the heat.

thermography A method of producing raised printing using regular ink and printing methods.

thesaurus A dictionary of synonyms and antonyms.

thin space A space that is defined as half the width of an en space.

third-party vendor A firm that markets an accessory hardware or software product for a given brand of computer equipment.

thirty-five character rule When selecting the line length or point size for text, a good rule of thumb to follow is the 35 character count. By this we mean that the average minimum character count for a line should be approximately 35 for optimum readability. A short measure containing considerably less than 35 characters per line will lead to excessive word breaks and hyphenations. Readability is lessened by the division of phrases and word groupings which disrupt the reading rhythm. In contrast, a long measure set with a small point size will have many characters, increasing the number of eye movements which can cause eye fatigue. Readability is also decreased. Due to the length, a reader may skip to the next line in midsentence or have difficulty in moving to the beginning of the new line.

threading Continuing a story through many columns, so that if you make a cut in the middle, it shrinks together from the end of the story.

three-dimensional graphics (3-D) A graphic image in three dimensions — height, width and depth. A three-dimensional image is rendered on a two-

shading or by means of perspective dimensional medium; the third dimension, depth, is usually indicated by shading or by means of perspective.

thumbnail A miniaturized version of a page showing the preliminary layout of a page. Used for laying out the page matrix in a publication.

tick mark Marks on the ruler that define increments for measuring.

TIFF An acronym for Tagged Image File Format, a standard format for recording bit mapped images on disk. TIFF files can store images of any size with any number of colors, using several kinds of data compression.

tight line A line of text that does not have enough extra space between words; dense appearance due to minimum wordspacing.

tiling The process of assembling more than one printed page, which, when put together, constitute an oversized publication; printing oversize pages with multiple overlapping sheets.

times backup A program feature that saves the file you are working on at specified intervals, such as every five minutes.

tint A percentage of a color or a shade of gray; an even tone area of a solid color created by screening.

tint block A graphic element of a mass of color placed behind type or art.

tint screen A uniform screen pattern used for visual effect in a layout.

tip-in The insertion of an additional page, by pasting, into a publication.

title (1) A book published by a book publisher. (2) The name of a specific publication.

title bar The line of text at the top of a window that indicates the name of the application or file in that window.

title page The first page of a book, or the third if there is a half-title page. It normally contains the title, author's name and publisher's imprint. It is always a right-hand (recto) page.

title section The first section in a book layout, containing such elements as the title page, frontispiece, table of contents, preface, etc. Same as *front matter*.

toggle (1) A keystroke that turns a function of a program on or off. (2) A device having two stable states. (3) The ability to go back and forth between two distinctly separate functions on a CRT.

tombstoning In page layout, the alignment of two identical looking objects beside each other. Tombstoning is generally considered to be poor design practice.

tone The strength of a color or shade of gray.

toner cartridge In a laser printer, the disposable container that holds the electrically charged dry ink (and sometimes a drum) used in creating an image on the paper. The dry ink (toner) is fused to paper in laser printing.

toolbox (1) A set of standard routines (pointing, cropping, drawing, etc.) provided by a program or operating system that can be called on by other programs or by the user. (2) An on-screen group of icons representing these routines.

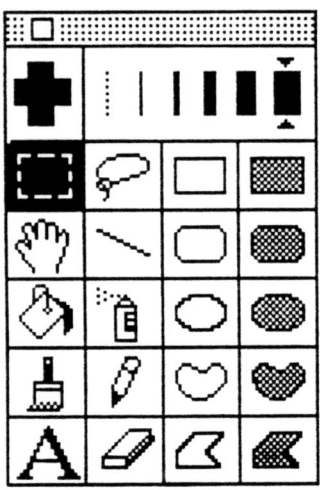

toolbox

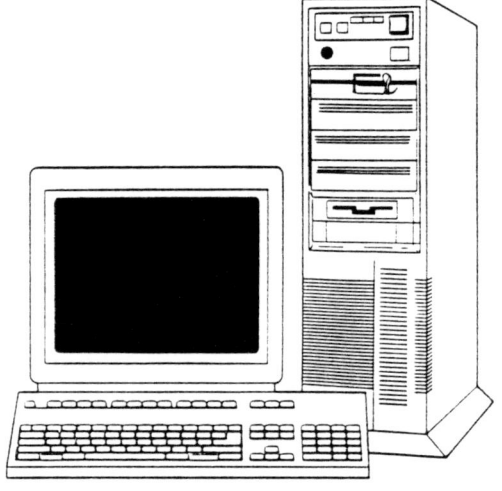

tower configuration

tower configuration A cabinet for a personal computer that is designed to stand upright on the floor with components stacked on top of each other. Tower cases usually have much more room for accessories.

track (1) Path along which data are recorded on a continuous or rotational medium, such as a magnetic disk. (2) To follow or record the moving position of a video display cursor, stylus, mouse, or other input device. (3) Reducing or increasing the letterspacing and wordspacing throughout a selection of text by a series of default values. Tracking shortens or lengthens the overall depth of the text.

trackball Device used to move the cursor around on a computer display screen. Consists of a mounting, usually a box, in which is set a ball. As the user spins the ball, the cursor moves at the speed and in the direction of the ball's motion. The housing is stationary, as opposed to the mobile mouse unit.

trackball

tracking (1) Moving a cursor or predefined symbol across the surface of the visual display screen with a light pen, electronic pen, trackball, or mouse. (2) The overall letterspacing in text. Tracking can also be used to tighten or loosen a block of type. Most publishing programs let you adjust tracking to accommodate spacing or appearance requirements.

tractor-feed mechanism Pair of pin-studded belts that rotate in unison and pull paper, punched with marginal holes, into a printer.

trademark A registered graphic or text and graphic element that identifies a company or product; a logo.

transient font A font which stays in the printer's memory until the current document is finished being printed.

transitional A type style which is characterized by moderate variations in stroke weight, smoothly-joined serifs, high contrast, and an almost vertical stress. First introduced in the late 18th century by John Baskerville.

trapped space White space that is completely surrounded by typographic elements.

trim marks Marks placed on a page to indicate the edge of the page.

trim size The final size of a printed piece.

truematch A color-matching system similar to Pantone.

TrueType A trademark for a high-level outline font technology developed by Apple Computer, Inc. TrueType provides scalable fonts to both the display screen and the printer. TrueType typefaces can be printed on any TrueType or PostScript compatible printer.

turnaround time The time it takes for a vendor to respond to your request for support or maintenance.

turnkey system Prepackaged ready-to-use computer system containing all the hardware, software, training, and maintenance support needed to perform a given application. All the prepared system needs is the "turn of the key." For example, a turnkey desktop publishing system might consist of a CPU, monitor, hard disk, scanner, laser printer and appropriate software. While easier to set up than off-the-shelf systems, equipment, training, and support choices are sometimes limited.

tutorial An instructional book or program that takes the user through a prescribed sequence of steps in order to learn a product.

TWAIN A cross-platform, interapplication interface standard that lets you use a scanner with any TWAIN-compatible application (such as Photoshop) rather than having to use an application dedicated to that particular.

two up Printing two pages side by side on a single sheet of paper.

type Refers to the text and or headline constituents of a document, as opposed to art and graphics. Includes numbers, letters, symbols and any and all characters.

typeface Collection of letters, numbers, and symbols that share a distinctive appearance. (e.g., Helvetica, Avant Garde, Times Roman, Bodoni, Schoolbook, Courier, and Palatino).

Avant Garde	Bodoni	Futura	Helvetica	Palatino
Berkeley	Courier	**Garamond**	Melior	Times

typeface

typeface family A group of typefaces that include the normal, bold, italic and bold-italic variations of the same design; a related group of type fonts.

Palatino *Palatino Oblique*
Palatino Bold ***Palatino Bold Oblique***

typeface family

Type 1 font PostScript outline font described using Adobe's hinting and encryption scheme, providing high quality at any size and any resolution.

typesetter Person who sets type using a phototypesetter or a desktop publishing system.

typesetting The production of camera-ready copy on a laser printer (low-quality typesetting) or an imagesetter (high-quality typesetting).

type size The height of a typeface measured in points.

8pt
9pt
10pt
11pt
12pt
14pt
16pt
18pt
20pt
22pt
24pt
30pt
36pt
45pt
72pt

type size

typestyle The weight (such as normal or bold) or posture (such as italic) of a font. See *typeface family*.

Roman *Italic* Book

 Reverse

type style

Type 3 font   User-defined font which can be described using most of the PostScript language to define the appearance of the character.

typo   A typographical error; typesetting or clerical error in setting type.

typography   The study and process of typefaces; how to select, size, arrange, and use them in general. Typography also includes computer display and output. Typography involves the planning, selecting, and setting of type for a printed work.

u&lc Abbreviation for capitals and small letters. A proofreader's mark for upper and lowercase letters.

ultraviolet coating Liquid applied to a printed sheet, then cured with ultraviolet (UV). UV coating has a high gloss and is more durable than varnish coating. It is used on book covers to protect the ink from rubbing off.

uncoated paper Paper that has not been coated with clay. Most business and book papers are uncoated papers. Uncoated paper is widely used for printing books, catalogs, flyers, direct-mail publications, etc.

uncorrected proof Photocopy of a book used as "advanced reading copy" for review in trade journals.

undelete A program feature that can restore a file that was accidentally erased from disk.

underrun A shortage of copies printed; less than the amount ordered.

underscore A rule directly below a line of type.

undo Command that undoes the effect of the previous command and puts the text or graphics back the way it was. Some programs provide multiple undo levels, letting you take back commands you gave in the past.

unity In graphic design, the combination of harmonious elements; size, color, shape, etc.

UNIX An easy-to-use operating system developed by Ken Thompson, Dennis Ritchie and coworkers at Bell Laboratories. Since the UNIX operating system is very easy to use, its design concept had a great influence on operating systems for microcomputers. UNIX is widely used on a great variety of computers, from mainframes to microcomputers.

unjustified text Text as it appears when typed on the display screen. It is not centered or justified. The same as *ragged right*.

unpublished Works that have not been distributed to the public.

update To modify a graphics file and make it reflect more recent information.

upgrade (1) To apply an enhancement or other improvement to a hardware or software component of an existing system. (2) To replace a software program with a more recently released version or a hardware device with one that provides better performance.

upload To transfer information (files) from some source to a host computer.

uppercase The large capital letters of a typeface. Text set in all capital letters.

upward compatible Term used to indicate that a computer system or peripheral device can do everything that the previous model could do, plus some additional functions. See compatibility.

user Any person authorized to operate any aspect of a computer graphics system.

user-friendly Term applied to software and/or hardware that has been designed to be easily used, without the user having to remember complex procedures. Very easy for the inexperienced person to use.

user group Group of computer users who share the knowledge they have gained and the programs they have developed on a computer or class of computers of a specific manufacturer. Usually meet to exchange information, share programs, and trade equipment.

user interface The features of a program or computer that govern the way it communicates with the person who is using it.

utility programs Computer programs that provide commonly needed services, such as performing mathematical functions or transferring data from one medium to another.

UV coating Liquid lamination dried by ultraviolet radiation, used as a protective coating for the printed piece, especially book covers. See *ultraviolet coating*.

vaccine An application program designed to counter the effects of a virus program.

value added reseller (VAR) Organizations that have licensed a product or products from an original manufacturer for resale under a new name by a different company.

vanity publisher See *subsidy publisher*.

variable leading Different amounts of space between lines.

variable space A space inserted by pressing the spacebar which might be of varying width to allow for justification of text.

varnishing Adding a varnish protective coating to the printed piece, especially a paperback book cover. It adds a shiny, hard surface to protect it.

VDT Acronym for Video Display Terminal, an input/output device consisting of a display screen and an input keyboard.

vector graphics A system of producing graphics using a limited number of "primitive" objects which can be resized, scaled, given color and tonal value and joined together to make complex graphics. Each primitive is an object such as a rectangle, oval, or line. See *object-oriented graphics*.

velox A halftone made on paper.

vendor Anyone who sells services or supports computer products for profit.

Ventura Publisher A desktop publishing program for IBM PC, IBM PS/2 and Apple Macintosh computers from Ventura Software, Inc. The program provides typeset-quality desktop publishing.

version Specific release of a software product of a specific hardware model. Usually numbered in ascending order. For example, DOS 6.0 is a later version of a disk operating system than is DOS 5.0 or DOS 4.1.

verso The left hand page of a book, opposite of recto.

vertical grid A series of vertical guidelines that help with alignment.

vertical justification The process of adding space between lines or paragraphs to achieve alignment of columns top and bottom.

vertical setting Type with letters over and under one another.

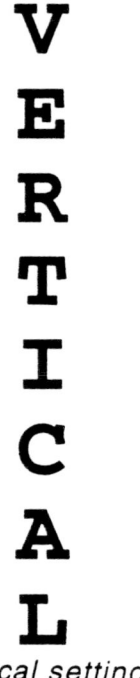

vertical setting

vertical ruler An electronic ruler displayed down the left side of a publication window.

VGA Acronym for Video Graphics Array. An IBM high-resolution video display standard for its personal computers. VGA displays images at 640 pixels horizontally by 480 pixels vertically. This color bit-mapped graphics display standard was introduced by IBM Corporation in 1987 with its Personal System/2 computer.

video adapter A plug-in circuit board that generates the output required to display computer text and graphics on a monitor.

video display terminal (VDT) Device for entering information into a computer system and displaying it on a screen. A typewriter-like keyboard is used to enter information.

video display terminal

view (1) To display information on a computer display screen. (2) The display of a graphical image from a given perspective. (3) In CAD programs, an image of a 3-D graphics model as it would be seen from a particular viewpoint. (4) In database systems, way of presenting the contents of a database to the user, not necessarily the same as the way the fields and records are stored in the database.

virgule The oblique line (/) used to separate one element from another in type.

virtual memory Storage that is actually provided on a disk drive or other mass storage device but appears to programs to be part of the main memory of the computer. Thus, the programs seem to use more main memory than is actually provided.

virus A computer program which can wreak havoc on a system, either by destroying data or simply gumming up the works. It is called a virus because it acts like a biological virus does in a human — the computer virus is not actually a live organism. Viruses usually enter via shareware or public domain programs, though there have been reports of viruses being carried by commercial software.

visual center The apparent center of a page, somewhat above the geometric center.

vortex Where the stems join at the lowest joint of a character, such as in the letters V and W. See *apex*.

weight The variation in the heaviness of a typeface. Common names for weights include light, demibold, and bold.

Light Regular **Bold Ultrabold**
weight

wf Abbreviation for wrong font, an indication that a letter of the wrong size or font has been set by mistake.

white space Literally, the white areas on a page which contribute to the overall composition. More or larger type implies less white space.

white space reduction The removal of equal amounts of space between letters in a line of type.

wholesaler A book distribution business that sells books to bookstores and libraries.

wide area network (WAN) Data communications network designed to serve an area of hundreds or thousands of miles. WAN's are generally implemented by linking together several remote Local Area Networks (LANs) through the use of gateways and bridges over dedicated telephone lines, satellite dishes or radio waves. See *local area network*.

wide page orientation See *landscape*.

widow A single word ending a paragraph. To be avoided.

window Portion of the video display area dedicated to some specific purpose. Special software allows the screen to be divided into multiple windows that can be moved around and made bigger or smaller. Windows allow the user to treat the computer display screen like a desktop where various flies can remain open simultaneously.

windowing software Programs that enable users to work with multiple on-screen windows. The Apple Macintosh Finder, Microsoft Windows and the

OS/2 Presentation Manager are all examples of windowing environments.

Windows A graphics-based operating environment for IBM-compatible microcomputers from Microsoft Corporation. It runs in conjunction with DOS. Some of the graphical user interface features include pull-down menus, multiple typefaces, desk accessories, and the capability of moving text and graphics from one program to another via a clipboard.

with the grain Folding paper parallel to the grain.

Word See *Microsoft Word*.

WordPerfect A popular, fully featured word processor introduced by WordPerfect Corporation in 1980.

word processing

word processing (WP) Technique for electronically storing, editing, and manipulating text by using an electronic keyboard, computer, and printer. The text is recorded on a magnetic medium, usually floppy disks. The final output is on paper. Words and letters are manipulated electronically, making it easy to copy and edit text.

windsurfing is fun   NORMAL WORDSPACING

windsurfing   is   fun   INCREASED WORDSPACING

word spacing

word spacing The spacing between words. It can be varied to adjust line length without affecting readability, unlike letterspacing.

WordStar A popular, full-featured word processing program introduced by WordStar International in 1978. It is available on IBM-compatible computers.

word wrap Feature that automatically moves a word to the beginning of the next line if it will not fit at the end of the original line. Feature found in word processing and page layout programs.

working title A preliminary title used while a book is in preparation.

workstation Configuration of computer equipment designed for use by one person at a time. This may have a terminal connected to a computer, or it may be a stand-alone system with local processing capability. Examples of workstations are a stand-alone system with local processing capability. Examples of workstations are a stand-alone graphics system, and a word processing system.

WORM An acronym for Write Once, Read Many times, which refers to a type of optical disk where a computer can save information once, then read that information, but cannot change it.

wrap A feature that positions text around a graphic image.

wraparound type Type that wraps around a graphic image in a body of text.

write (1) Process of transferring information from the computer to an output medium. (2) To record data in a storage device. Contrast with *read*.

write-protect (1) To mechanically prevent a 3.5-inch diskette from being written to. To write-protect a disk, move the write-protect tab so you can see through the Write-Protect Notch, or so the tab is at the bottom position in the notch. (2) 5.25-inch diskettes may be protected from the possibility of undesired recording of data by application of a gummed tab over the write-protect notch. An uncovered write-protect notch will allow writing to the diskette.

wysiwyg An acronym for What You See Is What You Get, a popular description for computer systems that supposedly always display upon the screen an accurate replica of what will eventually be transferred to hard copy.

XYZ

x-axis On a coordinate plane, the horizontal axis.

xerography The electrostatic process invented by Xerox in which an image is reflected onto an electrically charged drum which is then coated with similarly charged toner. The toner adheres to those parts of the drum where the image was reflected. Paper is rolled across the drum picking up a copy of the image and then passed through high temperature fusing rollers which melt the plastic based toner and fuse it to the paper.

x-height The height of lowercase letters without ascenders and descenders. It is a way of measuring type, it is the height of the lower case letter "x" in the particular font.

x-height

xylography One of the oldest and simplest methods of printing an illustration using a block of wood. Combined with typography, it led to the production of beautifully illustrated books at the end of the Middle Ages (14th to 15th centuries).

x-y plotter Output device that draws points, lines, or curves on a sheet of paper based on *x* and *y* coordinates from a computer.

x-y-z coordinate system A three-dimensional system of Cartesian coordinates that includes a third (*z*) axis running perpendicular to the horizontal (*x*) and vertical (*y*) axis.

y-axis On a coordinate plane, the vertical axis.

zap Erase, destroy or obliterate. Commonly used to describe deleting a file from disk storage.

Zapf Chancery A typeface developed by Hermann Zapf, a German typeface designer and owned by the International Typeface Corporation (ITC). The typeface is included as a built-in font with many PostScript laser printers.

abcdefghijklmnopqrstuvwxyz
ABCDEFGHIJKLMNOPQRSTUVWXYZ
1234567890 .,;:"&!?$

Zapf Chancery

Zapf Dingbats A set of decorative symbols developed by Hermann Zapf, a German typeface designer. Zapf Dingbats are used for decorative purposes in a document. The typeface is included as a built-in font with many PostScript laser printers.

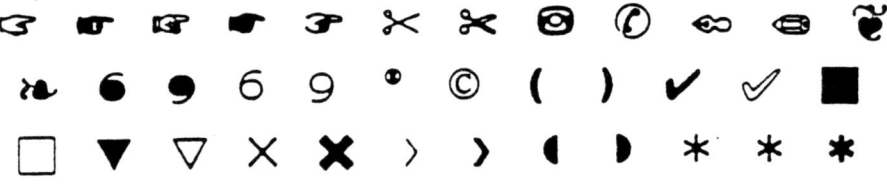

Zapf Dingbats

z-axis On a coordinate plane, the axis that represents depth.

zooming Changing of a view on a graphics display by either moving in on successively smaller portions of the currently visible picture or moving out until the window encloses the entire scene.

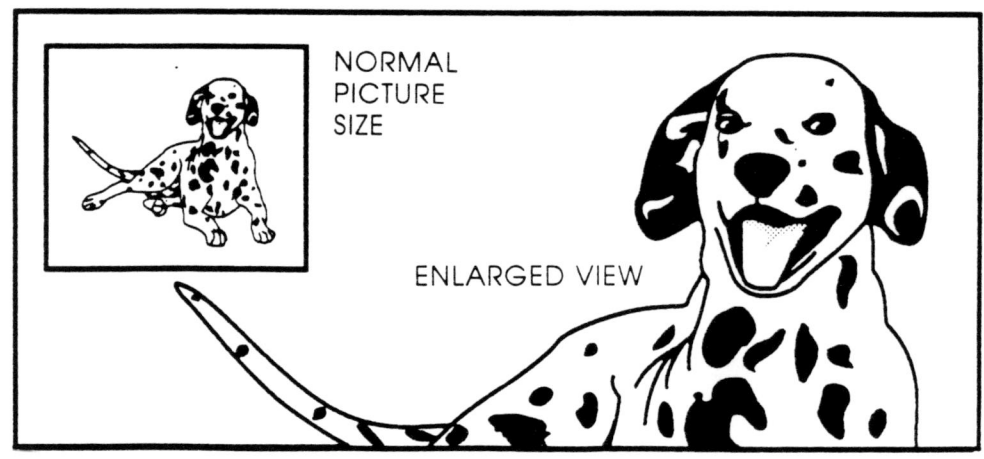

zooming